The Language of Literature:

An Introduction to Stylistics

Marcello Giovanelli and Jessica Mason

Series Editors: Dan Clayton and Marcello Giovanelli

CAMBRIDGE
UNIVERSITY PRESS

University Printing House, Cambridge CB2 8BS, United Kingdom

One Liberty Plaza, 20th Floor, New York, NY 10006, USA

477 Williamstown Road, Port Melbourne, VIC 3207, Australia

314–321, 3rd Floor, Plot 3, Splendor Forum, Jasola District Centre, New Delhi – 110025, India

79 Anson Road, #06–04/06, Singapore 079906

Cambridge University Press is part of the University of Cambridge.

It furthers the University's mission by disseminating knowledge in the pursuit of education, learning and research at the highest international levels of excellence.

www.cambridge.org
Information on this title: www.cambridge.org/9781108402217

First published 2018

20   19   18   17   16   15   14   13   12   11   10   9   8   7   6   5   4   3   2

Printed in Great Britain by CPI Group (UK) Ltd, Croydon CR0 4YY

A catalogue record for this publication is available from the British Library

ISBN 978-1-108-40221-7 Paperback

Contents

Series introduction

Cambridge Topics in English Language is a series of accessible introductory study guides to major scholarly topics in the fields of English language and linguistics. These books have been designed for use by students at advanced level and beyond and provide detailed overviews of each topic together with the latest research in the field so as to provide a clear introduction that is both practical and up to date.

In all of the books in this series, we have drawn on examples of spoken and written language. We hope these will encourage you to apply the theories, concepts and methods that you will learn in the books to analyse data and to think critically about a number of issues and debates relating to language in use. Many of the books also draw on data from the Cambridge Corpus. Throughout each book, you will find short activities to help develop reading and writing skills, longer extended activities and practice questions that will enable you to explore your learning in more detail and research findings that will provide inspiration for your own language investigations. Each of the chapters includes suggested wider reading, and a full glossary and reference section at the end of each book will support you to extend your learning and provide avenues for future reading and research.

We hope that each book will give you a good overview of its topic and, that taken as a whole, the series will map out some of the most interesting and diverse areas of language study, providing you with fresh thinking and new ideas as you embark on your studies.

Dan Clayton

Marcello Giovanelli

How to use this book

Throughout this book you will notice recurring features that are designed to help your learning. Here is a brief overview of what you'll find.

Coverage list

A short list of what you will learn in each chapter.

KEY TERM

Definitions of important terms to help your understanding of the topic.

ACTIVITY

A clearly defined task to help you apply what you've learnt.

RESEARCH QUESTION

A longer task to help you go deeper into the topic.

PRACTICE QUESTION

To give you some practice of questions you might encounter in the exam.

Ideas and answers

Further information, suggestions and answers to all activities and practice questions in the book.

Wider reading

Key texts to help extend your learning.

Topic introduction

This is a book about studying literature. It is a book that takes the approach that the best way to study literary texts is by focusing closely on the language of those texts: the choices and patterns made by an author as a way of exploring how readers might respond and how they might form interpretations.

The academic discipline we both work in is known as stylistics and this book aims to provide you with a basic introduction to the field. Stylistics is concerned with how texts are written, read and evaluated by readers in a number of different contexts. We have tried to show the versatility of a stylistics approach by drawing on texts from different literary genres, by showing you a range of established methods that form the 'stylistician's toolkit' and by highlighting some more recent work in the field such as cognitive stylistics and working with reader responses. We have provided wider reading suggestions for you at the end of each chapter that we hope you will find useful.

Finally, we would argue that the best way to understand stylistics is to do stylistics. We encourage you therefore to explore texts in the light of the ideas presented in this book and to try out the methods mapped out in each of the chapters. We hope that you will find a language-focused approach to literary texts an exciting and enabling one!

Marcello Giovanelli

Jessica Mason

Chapter 1
What is stylistics?

In this chapter you will:

- Be introduced to the discipline of stylistics

- Understand the main principles of stylistic analysis

- Explore the advantages of adopting a stylistic approach to literature

1

1.1 Introduction

In this chapter you will be introduced to the discipline of stylistics and explore how it differs from other approaches to analysing literature. The chapter will outline the main principles of stylistics and consider the benefits of this approach.

1.2 Defining stylistics

Stylistics is a discipline within the field of linguistics. This means that it is a particular application of knowledge about language, just like sociolinguistics (the study of language in social use) or psycholinguistics (the study of the psychology of language). Stylistics, as the name suggests, is interested in style in spoken and written language. It is underpinned by the idea that whenever we use language to talk or write, we are always – consciously and unconsciously – making choices about the words we use (lexical choices) and the order in which we use them (syntactic structure). These choices form a particular style and changing the choices changes the style. This is what stylistics explores: how authors create effects through their linguistic styles and how readers interpret those effects. Stylistics is thus 'simply defined as the (linguistic) study of style, which is the way in which language is used' (Leech and Short 2007: 1).

KEY TERMS

Stylistics: the study of style; a discipline within the field of linguistics that examines how every linguistic choice can influence the overall effect of a text

Lexical choices: choosing a particular word or phrase

Syntactic structure: the structure of a sentence

ACTIVITY 1.1

Style as choice

Consider the two versions of the haiku in Text 1A and Text 1B. How, in your view, have the distinct lexical choices changed the style of the text?

You might find it interesting to return to this activity at the end of the book and see how much you have learned.

Text 1A

A tiger can smile

A snake will say it loves you

Lies make us evil

Extract from *Fight Club*, Chuck Palahniuk (1996)

Text 1B

The tiger may smile

The snake might say it loves you

Lies make us evil?

In this book you'll be looking at stylistics and literature, but it's worth noting right from the start that stylistics can be used to analyse and explore *any* text. This is because, as you'll see in more detail in section 1.4 ('Principles of stylistics'), stylisticians believe that there is no fundamental difference between literature and any other kind of text, even spoken conversations, because all 'texts' are made up of language.

Stylistics has its roots in rhetoric, dating all the way back to Ancient Greece and, later, Rome. Rhetoric was centrally concerned with exploring and examining the effects of language and how particular choices could make a speech more, or less, persuasive and compelling. The Greeks' interest in rhetoric began because, if you were accused of a crime in those days, you were not allowed to hire a lawyer or have someone else speak in your defence: you were required to speak for yourself. As such, a vested interest in speaking persuasively and effectively sprang up all over the country. The Romans, later picked up and developed the Greek interest in rhetoric, and so the rhetorical tradition was born. Today, stylistics mirrors this focus on examining the effects of language.

Stylistics inherited something else from the rhetorical tradition too: a central focus on the use of metalanguage. Metalanguage is best defined as terms we use to describe language itself, especially particular linguistic features such as nouns, verbs, similes, metaphors, and so on. If you'd like to find out more about rhetoric, and the many hundreds of items of metalanguage coined by this tradition, the best place is the fantastic website *Silva Rhetoricae: The Forest of Rhetoric*, at www.cambridge.org/links/esclit6001, run by Brigham Young University.

Metalanguage is important for transparency and clarity: if I label a word as a noun, or a determiner, or I say something is a metaphor, and we're both agreed on the definition of that specific term, it means that you are able to judge whether or not you agree with me. This is vitally important: if instead, I use a more impressionistic word and it is ambiguous what I might mean, then it becomes very difficult for anyone to disagree with me. Paul Simpson (2014: 6) offers an excellent illustration of this when he describes being at a talk and hearing a critic refer to a writer's style as 'invertebrate'. Simpson explains that, even if this feels like a good adjective with which to describe a writer's style, it doesn't really mean anything. Does invertebrate mean fluid and flexible, or does it mean weak and spineless? The lack of clarity makes the claim effectively unchallengeable. As such, stylisticians believe clear, consistent and precise use of metalanguage must be a fundamental part of any text analysis.

> ## KEY TERMS
> **Rhetoric:** the art and study of effective or persuasive speaking or writing
>
> **Metalanguage:** terminology used to describe language features

In more recent years, stylistics has undergone an evolution commonly referred to as 'the cognitive turn', reflecting an explosion of knowledge about language and the mind (Gavins and Steen 2003; Stockwell 2002). As a result, a significant strand of research involving the 'application of cognitive science to literary reading' (Stockwell 2012), sometimes called 'cognitive poetics', has developed (Gavins and Steen 2003; Stockwell 2002). Cognitive poetics is a discipline which borrows from many others, including psychology, cognitive science and neuroscience. Cognitive poetics adopts the position that 'literature does not exist unless it is read' (Stockwell 2012). You will have the opportunity to explore this branch of stylistics in detail in Chapter 4 ('Stylistics and the mind').

1.3 Why stylistics?

So why should you adopt a stylistic approach to your literary analysis?

In many ways, stylistics is a discipline which emerged in the middle of the twentieth century as a reaction to what many perceived as the vague and impressionistic nature of much literary criticism, of the kind demonstrated in the example above. As an approach, it offers an ideal balance between your own interpretation of a text and close reference to the language to support your analysis.

A metaphor frequently engaged to characterise the stylistic approach is the idea of a 'stylistics toolkit' (Leech and Short 2007; Wales 2014). Katie Wales argues that stylistics is a discipline which is 'hands-on' and 'requires 'spade-work', which is 'the systematic close reading and analysis of quite specific elements' (Wales

2014: 32–3). Stylistics is democratic and liberating in this sense: the 'toolkit' is comprised of frameworks, theories and models, all of which use clear and specific metalanguage, and once a person has mastered those terms, everyone is on an even footing. It doesn't matter whether you've been a stylistician for weeks, months or years – we all use the same terms so we are all able to assess and critique each other's analyses.

The emphasis on using clearly defined metalanguage within the toolkit thus creates 'a common currency of technical terminology' (Stockwell and Whiteley 2014: 5). This ensures that all the stages of any analysis are open to scrutiny by other researchers in the field: an agreed vocabulary means that interpretations are disputable because it is clear how they were reached. Peter Stockwell (2012) explains: 'an emphasis on textual evidence […] ensures that claims made are open to agreement or falsifiability, are open to verification and checking for accuracy, and are fundamentally testable'.

Stylistics sits between language and literature, seeing them as closely related and mutually dependent. That is, it neither asks you to label linguistic forms and features in a text for the sake of it – a practice often negatively referred to as feature spotting – nor does it allow you to make sweeping claims about literary interpretation without grounding it in textual evidence.

KEY TERM

Feature spotting: labelling features in a text with metalanguage with no further comment or any reference to the effects that feature creates; a practice to be avoided

---

1.4 Principles of stylistics

Paul Simpson (2014: 4) explains that stylistics can be thought about as conforming to the following three basic principles, cast mnemonically as three 'Rs'. The three Rs stipulate that:

Stylistic analysis should be **rigorous**.

Stylistic analysis should be **retrievable**.

Stylistic analysis should be **replicable**.

This means that stylisticians present literary analyses by showing all their working out. The analysis will be 'rigorous' in the sense that it will look holistically at a text and not cherry-pick particular examples which suit the argument the stylistician would like to make. If a stylistician calls something *invertebrate* – like the critic in Simpson's example above – they define what they mean and point to evidence in the text to support their claim. This means that the analysis is also 'retrievable': you can see how all interpretations have been reached – the logic and reasoning as to how those interpretations have been reached is explicit and explained. In other words, there is full transparency – at no point do you have to guess how or why a conclusion has been reached, nor do you have to 'take the analyst's word for it' that their point is accurate, because you can see it for yourself. Thus, too, the analysis will be 'replicable': if you were to take the same text and apply the same tools from the stylistics toolkit, you too should be able to draw the same conclusions.

Wider reading

You can find out more about the topics in this chapter by reading the following:

Gavins, J. and Steen, G. (2003) *Cognitive Poetics in Practice*. London: Routledge.

Leech, G. and Short, M. (2007) *Style in Fiction* (Second Edition). London: Longman.

Simpson, P. (2014) *Stylistics: A Resource Book for Students* (Second Edition). London: Routledge.

Stockwell, P. (2002) *Cognitive Poetics: An Introduction*. London: Routledge.

Stockwell, P. and Whiteley, S. (eds) (2014) *The Cambridge Handbook of Stylistics*. Cambridge: Cambridge University Press.

Chapter 2
Developing a stylistics toolkit

In this chapter you will:

- Explore the idea of foregrounding in stylistics

- Develop a range of tools and methods to support the analysis of literary texts

- Develop your ability to write about texts in an enabling manner

2.1 Introduction

In this chapter, you will look at how you can develop your own toolkit to enable you to explore and analyse texts. Although the focus of this book is on the stylistic analysis of literary fiction, the knowledge and skills that you will develop will also help you to analyse other kinds of texts. This chapter will give you a set of tools and methods that you can use as you explore texts and develop your skills as a stylistician.

The chapter begins with a discussion of foregrounding, a central concept in stylistics, and one that will be returned to and referred to throughout this book. Following that, there is a focus on words, structures and sounds. Each of these sections is designed to give you a good foundation from which you can analyse literary texts with precision and confidence. The aim of section 2 is to provide you with a basic toolkit which you can extend by following up further reading suggestions and by working through the later chapters of this book where more specific tools and methods will be introduced to support your work.

> ### KEY TERM
> **Foregrounding:** the act of giving some textual features prominence to suggest they have a significant influence on meaning

2.2 Foregrounding

2.2.1 What is foregrounding?

One of the most important concepts in stylistics is the notion of foregrounding. It has its roots in very early work in stylistics and is particularly influenced by Russian formalism, a literary movement in the early twentieth century that attempted to identify as precisely as possible the key features of literary texts and by doing so account for their unique properties. Formalist analyses focused on the power of literature to present something in a striking and/or unexpected way so as to make it stand out and demand a reader's attention. The Russian formalists argued that foregrounding worked through a process of defamiliarisation.

Foregrounding is a very important term for stylistics since it provides a basis for thinking about how both individual words and groups of words help to construct meaning. It emphasises how meaning is dependent on patterns that are built up through individual word choices and highlights how language can be viewed as a system where the choices writers and speakers make are highly significant since they necessarily exclude other potential choices.

A useful way of understanding foregrounding is through a visual analogy. Typically our visual field organises objects and space into a structured relationship where one thing stands out against everything else that remains in the background. Figure 2.1 shows a very basic example of this.

Figure 2.1: Foreground and background

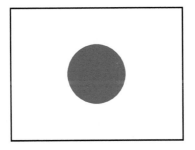

In Figure 2.1, the red dot is foregrounded as a result of its colour (it is brighter) and its size (it is more defined and smaller than the white space). Consequently, attention is drawn to the foregrounded object. In general, foregrounded objects may stand out through being a different colour, being more sharply defined, being in motion, and so on. In many instances, this foregrounding results in very clear effects and can have obvious benefits: for example, if you are waiting to cross the road, a moving car coming towards you will stand out against the static background of the road. This will generally mean that you will avoid stepping out into its path! Foregrounding can therefore be viewed as an attention-grabbing strategy and, of course, writers and speakers can make use of this to emphasise ideas they want their readers and listeners to interpret as being significant.

In written texts, foregrounding occurs either through:

- the formation of patterns, known as parallelism, and/or

- the breaking of patterns, known as deviation.

KEY TERMS

Parallelism: the setting up of textual patterns at any language level

Deviation: the breaking of textual patterns at any language level

---

Text 2A and Text 2B illustrate this. In Text 2A, the opening to Kenneth Fearing's poem 'Evening song', parallelism occurs through the repeated imperative form (an order) at the beginning of each line.

Text 2A

Sleep, McKade.

Fold up the day. It was a bright scarf.

Put it away.

Take yourself to pieces like a house of cards.

> Extract from 'Evening song', Kenneth Fearing (1927)

Text 2B is the opening lines to William Wordsworth's poem 'Resolution and independence'. Here, poetic deviation occurs in the third line, which provides a contrast both in structure (the line begins with 'but') and themes (sun against wind and rain, calmness against noise, upwards movement against downwards movement) to the harsh stormy weather outlined in the first two lines.

Text 2B

There was a roaring in the wind all night;

The rain came heavily and fell in floods;

But now the sun is rising calm and bright;

> Extract from 'Resolution and independence', William Wordsworth (1807)

2.2.2 Foregrounding explored

For an extended example of how parallelism and deviation work in literary fiction, look at Text 2C, the opening to 'Why don't you dance?', a short story by the American author Raymond Carver (numbers have been added to each of the sentences).

Text 2C

In the kitchen, he poured another drink and looked at the bedroom suite in his front yard. (1)

The mattress was stripped and the candy-striped sheets lay beside two pillows on the chiffonier. (2)

Except for that, things looked pretty much the way they had in the bedroom – nightstand and reading lamp on his side of the bed, nightstand and reading lamp on her side. (3)

His side, her side. (4)

He considered this as he sipped the whisky. (5)

Extract from 'Why don't you dance?', Raymond Carver, Knopf (2009)

Although foregrounding can occur at any level of language analysis, in this example we will focus on the effects achieved through sentence patterning. As you can see, the extract contains five sentences. Four of these are multi-clause sentences (containing more than one main verb) while one is a minor sentence (has no main verb at all).

1 Multi-clause

2 Multi-clause

3 Multi-clause

4 Minor

5 Multi-clause

According to foregrounding theory, these parallel multi-clause structures will invite a reader to draw some meaningful connection between them.

In sentence 1, the first clause describes an action in the family home while the second clause disrupts any expectations about houses and furniture by depicting the bedroom suite as being 'in the front yard' when it would normally be expected to be inside the house. In the second sentence, the two phrases, one embedded in the other 'beside two pillows on the chiffonier' present a similar kind of dislocation (sheets and pillows should be on the bed) to that of the bedroom suite in the first sentence. The parallel structures therefore foreground an emphasis on place and contrast.

This foregrounding continues in sentence 3, where the clauses refer to and bring together the positioning of the bedroom furniture both remembered inside the house and now positioned outside. Equally, sentence 5 brings together the two contrasting states of thought 'considered' and action 'sipped'. The sentences foreground the central theme of contrast between spatial and mental states.

2.2.3 Deviation explored

Deviation can occur in one of two ways:

- external deviation, where conventional and expected ways of communicating are flouted, for example in the use of nonsense words or the use of an inappropriate register for a particular genre

- the more common internal deviation, where a pattern in the *text itself* is broken.

In the Carver extract, there are examples of internal deviation. The minor sentence 4 deviates from the main sentence pattern in the text to suggest a timeless, abstract state. In addition, the parallel phrases, 'His side, her side,' are a further more fine-tuned type of foregrounding, which could be interpreted in a number of ways. A plausible interpretation might be that the minor sentence provides a stark reminder for the main character (and the reader) of the distance that now exists between the former partners.

KEY TERMS

External deviation: deviation that breaks from the normal conventions of language use, for example in the use of nonsense words or ungrammatical constructions

Internal deviation: deviation that breaks from a pattern that has previously been set up in the text for a striking effect

---

Finally, further patterns of parallelism and deviation can be traced in the focus of the five sentences. Sentences 1–4 set up a pattern of inwards movement, from the bedroom suite, to the mattress, sheets and pillows, to the nightstand and reading lamp, to the striking and climactic opposition of separated former lovers in the minor sentence. The final sentence deviates from this pattern by returning to a focus on the main character's thoughts and actions, which are now foregrounded and consequently return to the reader's attention.

A further interesting type of foregrounding can involve representing a character's speech by using elements of regional and/or non-Standard English. Read Text 2D, from the opening of Clare Wigfall's short story 'Night after night'.

Text 2D

I was peeling the potatoes for our tea when the sweep of bright headlights across the kitchen window caught me eye. 'Look at that, love,' I called out to him in the front room, 'coppers in the courtyard.' And I stood up on me toes, leaning against the sink to try to get a better view.

Thinking on it now, I suppose it was a bit peculiar that he didn't say nothing back to me nor get up from his chair to have a look. Stan just turned off his radio show and finished up his cup of tea and sat there waiting, as if he knew it was our bell they was going to ring.

Extract from 'Night after night', Clare Wigfall, Faber (2007)

In this extract, the narrator uses several non-standard forms: 'me' instead of 'my' to show possession, a double negative 'didn't say nothing' instead of 'didn't say anything', and 'was' instead of 'were'. These non-standard features might suggest an older character using a regional variety of English, possibly in the London area (the use of 'love' and 'copper' are typically associated with the dialect spoken by older speakers in London). They are foregrounded in the sense that they deviate from Standard English, and are thus highlighted as an essential part of the narrator's character: a down-to-earth, straight-talking and rather homely type.

Finally, another common type of deviation is where an author manipulates the conventions of text design. Read Text 2E, 'Wind', a poem by Eugen Gomringer.

Text 2E

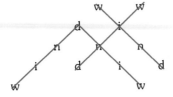

In this poem, Gomringer dramatically deviates from the expected conventions of writing. The four instances of 'wind' read in straight lines (shown in red) to convey the direction from where the wind blows (north, south, east and west). This in itself of course forms a pattern and foregrounds an interpretation and yet it is also possible to read wind in (and as) a series of winding chains (three of which are shown in blue), this time emphasising the random and changing nature of the wind's force.

'Wind' is considered to be an example of concrete poetry, a genre that became very popular in the 1950s and 1960s and which relied heavily on typographical features and visual design to generate effects and meaning. You could explore how foregrounding (both parallelism and deviation) operates in this genre by looking at these poems.

- George Herbert (1633) 'Easter wings'

- e.e. cummings (1923) 'in Just-'

- May Swenson (1994) 'Stone gullets'

- Lorna Dee Cervantes (1997) 'Valentine'

- Brook Emery (2007) 'Very like a whale'

ACTIVITY 2.1

Exploring foregrounding

Foregrounding can occur at any of the language levels that are explored in more detail in sections 2.4–2.6:

- Words (section 2.4): use of unusual lexical choices, non-standard or taboo language for effect, repetition of individual words or words from a particular semantic field.

- Structure (section 2.5): the use of unusual or non-standard word order and sentence patterns.

- Sounds (section 2.6): rhyme, various types of sound symbolism.

You might want to work through these sections before looking at this activity.

Take a short extract from a poem or a short story. Find examples of foregrounded language features both in terms of parallelism and deviation. Can you find a text or extract, as with Text 2C, where both parallelism and deviation occur? For each example that you find, explain what you think are the interpretative effects of foregrounding.

2.3 Using levels of language analysis

The principle of foregrounding is crucial to stylistic analysis since it highlights that patterns in language influence how we make meaning. It's also a principle that can be applied to any of the ways that we can divide up the study of language. For example, you have already looked at foregrounding at the level of visual design, word choice and sentence structure. In the following sections, you will use this principle as you develop your 'toolkit' by considering the three key levels of language analysis in more detail.

2.4 Words

The study of words involves exploring lexis and semantics. In this section, the focus is on how words can be divided into types to provide a way of categorising language more accurately and usefully, and on how words can be explored to form cohesive structures that give meanings across larger stretches of text.

KEY TERMS

Lexis: the term used to refer to the vocabulary system

Semantics: the study of meaning in language

2.4.1 Word classes

A word class is a group of words that have shared characteristics and functions in speech and writing. The main word classes are:

- Noun: names a person, thing or concept, e.g. *John, carpet, love*

- Verb: shows a state of being, action or event (we can call this a process), e.g. *be, go, think, say*

- Adjective: modifies a noun, e.g. _big_ house, _dark_ night, _spectacular_ event

- Adverb: modifies a verb, adjective or another adverb, e.g. ran _quickly_, _very_ small, _quite_ suddenly

- Pronoun: substitutes for a noun, often referring back or forwards to them, e.g. _he, she, they, it_

- Determiner: adds detail or clarity to nouns, e.g. _the, my, some_

- Preposition: provides connections between words, often showing a sense of place or time, e.g. _in, on, between, during_

- Conjunction: provides connections between the larger structures: phrases, clauses and sentences, e.g. _and, but, because._

KEY TERMS

Noun: a word that names a thing or concept

Verb: a word that shows a state of being, action or event

Adjective: a word that modifies a noun

Adverb: a word that modifies a verb, an adjective or another adverb

Pronoun: a word that substitutes for a noun

Determiner: a word that adds detail or clarity to a noun

Preposition: a word that shows connections between other words often showing a sense of place or time

Conjunction: a word that connects larger structures such as phrases, clauses and sentences

Most word classes can also be further broken down into sub-types. Table 2.1 shows how we can sub-classify each of the word classes discussed above.

Table 2.1: Sub-classes

Nouns

Sub-class	Description	Examples
Proper	Refer to names of people or places	James, England
Abstract	Refer to states, feelings and concepts that do not have a physical existence	love, anger
Concrete (countable and non-countable)	Refer to objects that have a physical existence	countable (can be pluralised), e.g. cup(s)
		non-countable (do not take a plural form), e.g. furniture

Verbs

Sub-class	Description	Examples
Material	Show actions or events	hit, jump, wash, build
Relational	Identify properties or show states of being	be, appear, seem, become
Mental	Show internal processes such as thinking	think, believe, wish
Verbal	Show external processes of communicating through speech	say, shout, scream, whisper

Adjectives and adverbs

Sub-class	Description	Examples
Base	The basic form of an adjective or adverb, modifying another word	(adjective) big, interesting (adverb) carefully
Comparative	A form used to compare two instances by adding 'er' or using 'more'	The parcel was bigger. That was a more interesting game. He read more carefully
Superlative	A form used to compare more than two instances, identifying a best example	That was the biggest parcel. The most interesting game. It was the most carefully he had ever read

Pronouns

Sub-class	Description	Examples
Personal	Refer to people and are differentiated in terms of person (first, second, third), number (singular or plural) and gender (male or female)	I (first-person singular/ plural), you (second-person singular/plural), she (third-person singular, feminine), they (third person plural)
Demonstrative	Orientate the reader or listener towards a person, object or idea, either nearby or further away	this, these, that, those
Indefinite	Refer to a person, object or idea that is non-specific	someone, anybody, everything

Determiners

Sub-class	Description	Examples
Articles	Show that something is definite or indefinite	the (definite) a/an (indefinite)
Possessives	Show ownership	my, your, her, our
Quantifiers	Show either specific or non-specific quantities of a noun	one, two (specific) some, any, a few (non-specific)

Prepositions

Sub-class	Description	Examples
Single	Consist of one word	in, through, with, on
Complex	Consist of two or more words	according to, because of, on top of, next to
Postpositions	Follow their complements in a prepositional phrase	ago, apart, aside

Conjunctions

Sub-class	Description	Examples
Co-ordinating	Link words or larger structures such as phrases and clauses together where they are equal	and, but, or, yet
Sub-ordinating	Link clauses together to show one is dependent on another	because, although, while, for

A good knowledge of the different types of word class is important since, as a stylistician, you will need to be able to label language features precisely and comment on the interpretative significance of patterns that you can see. As an example, let's look at Text 2F, an extract from Susan Hill's novella *The Small Hand*. In this extract, taken from near the beginning of the story, the narrator is describing arriving at an abandoned house.

Text 2F

I touched the cold iron latch. It lifted. I pushed. The gate was stuck fast. I put my shoulder to it and it gave a little and rust flaked away at the hinges. I pushed harder and slowly the gate moved, scraping on the ground, opening, opening. I stepped through it and I was inside. Inside a large, overgrown, empty, abandoned garden. To one side, steps led to a terrace and the house.

Extract from *The Small Hand*, Susan Hill, Profile Books (2010)

The main word classes in this extract can be identified as follows:

- **Nouns:** latch, gate, shoulder, rust, hinges, gate, ground, garden, steps, terrace, house
- **Verbs:** touched, lifted, pushed, was, gave, flaked away, moved, scraping, opening, stepped, was, led
- **Adjectives:** cold, iron, stuck fast, inside, large, overgrown, empty, abandoned
- **Adverbs:** harder, slowly
- **Pronouns:** I, it
- **Determiners:** the, my, a, one
- **Prepositions:** to, at, through
- **Conjunctions:** and

As you can see, nouns and verbs appear more frequently than other word classes. This is expected since, in prose fiction, these are the word classes that set out the parameters of the fictional world, encouraging us to conceptualise characters, locations and events. You will also see some clear patterns emerging in the specific sub-types of word class that Hill uses. For example, the nouns used are common nouns that indicate place: the gate, the garden and the house. The verbs in this extract are largely material processes, representing actions carried out or associated with the narrator of the story. Interestingly, these move from being narrator-centred to being associated with the gate itself, which despite being an inanimate object is given a sense of agency (it moves, scrapes and opens), perhaps adding to the suspense and supernatural feel of the extract.

Among the other word classes, there are some additional important patterns. The use of the first-person pronoun 'I' throughout anchors the point of view to one narrating character. The first set of adjectives in the extract is centred on the gate, emphasising its prominence, while the second set modify the noun 'garden'. It is interesting to note that Hill uses four adjectives in her description of the garden, which combine to present a richly defined image for the reader. Finally, Hill uses both the indefinite article 'a' and the definite article 'the'. Since the difference between the two is often one of accessibility (a writer or speaker will tend to use 'the' when the noun following is either well-known or has been mentioned before), this raises some interesting possible interpretative effects.

2.4.2 Semantics: meaning relations

You can see in the discussion above that patterns in word classes may give rise to particular interpretations and meanings. In fact, many of the patterns discussed in relation to *The Small Hand* can also be explored through the lens of semantics, the study of how meanings are formed.

One way of capturing how meanings are formed is to look at how words combine with other words. A collection of words that are based around a topic or theme are said to be part of the same semantic field.

KEY TERM

Semantic field: a group of words that fulfil the same kind of role and function in speech and writing

---

In the extract from *The Small Hand*, there are a group of words that are related in so far as they all form part of a lexical set describing a landscape/property. Words within this set also have additional semantic relationships. For example, 'latch' and 'hinges' are all parts of a gate. Using these terms avoids both repetition of 'gate' and makes the narrative scene more specific: the narrator adds finer detail that enables the reader to more precisely visualise the specific part of the gate being mentioned. In this instance, the part-whole relationship that exists between the words 'latch' and 'gate' is known as meronymy.

In general, the meaning of a word can often be discussed in relation to how it relates to other words in the vocabulary system. One such relationship is between synonyms, words that have largely equivalent meanings. Some synonyms such as 'quick' and 'fast' may be used fairly interchangeably, whilst in other situations various contextual factors may influence the choice of one word over another. For example, 'lavatory' and 'toilet' are synonyms (they refer to the same entity) but the difference in formality (high versus low) means that their use is likely to be governed by the audience and/or purpose of speaking or writing. Of course, in literary fiction, the choice of one synonym over another is likely to be highly significant as is the decision to use synonymous – or near synonymous – words following each other. For example, in the extract from *The Small Hand*, 'empty' and 'abandoned' are near synonyms and together foreground, through semantic parallelism, the rundown state of the garden. However, the repetition highlights a subtle distinction in meaning: the use of 'abandoned' foregrounds a human agent responsible for leaving the garden in this way.

In contrast to synonyms, antonyms are words that have opposite meanings. Some antonyms are complete opposites or complementary, such as 'alive' and 'dead' (a person can only be one or the other), whilst others are gradable, such as 'long' and 'short' (something could conceivably be quite short or quite long). Again, the strategic use of antonyms in literary fiction can produce interesting interpretative effects. For example, when reading the extract from *The Small Hand*, you might wonder whether a garden can be both 'overgrown' and 'empty'? Again, the use of near antonyms invites the reader to examine the semantic subtleties of each word in the context in which it is used.

KEY TERMS

Meronymy: a relationship between words that have a part-whole structure

Synonymy: a relationship where words have largely equivalent meanings

Antonymy: a relationship where words have opposite meanings

A final meaning relation, hyponomy, describes how a more general overarching term encapsulates more specific examples. For example, 'house' is a specific example of 'building' but can also be a more general term for particular kinds of houses such as 'summerhouse', 'playhouse', bungalow', and so on. Hyponomy can be viewed as a kind of semantic chain along which more or less specific words that are all semantically related exist. A higher word in the chain is seen to be superordinate to a lower-level, subordinate one.

> KEY TERM
>
> **Hyponomy:** a relationship between words where one word is a more specific instance of a more general term

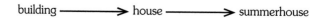

building ⟶ house ⟶ summerhouse

2.4.3 Semantics: cohesion

As we have seen, relationships between words may act as a kind of foregrounding that provides cohesion and allows the reader to identify key thematic concerns and make connections between lexical and semantic features. There are, however, some additional kinds of cohesion that occur in texts.

Anaphoric referencing involves using another word (usually a pronoun) to refer back to a previously used word that has already established a mental representation of a concept or thing (the referent). In this example, the pronoun 'It' refers back to the noun 'latch'.

I touched the cold iron latch. It lifted.

A second type, cataphoric referencing, occurs when the referent comes *after* the pronoun. For example, the two sentences could have read:

I touched it. The cold iron latch lifted.

> KEY TERMS
>
> **Anaphoric referencing:** using a word (usually a pronoun) to refer back to a previous, different word so as to create cohesion
>
> **Referent:** the concept or thing referred to by a word
>
> **Cataphoric referencing:** using a word (usually a pronoun) that refers to another word that follows later

In this rewriting, the pronoun 'it' anticipates its referent 'latch'. Of course, you might also think how you interpret the original text. Does delaying the referent affect how you process the narrative?

ACTIVITY 2.2

Words and interpretations

Take a short extract from a literary text of your choice. Identify the different word classes used and comment on any patterns that you find. For example, what types of nouns and verbs dominate? Can you relate this to the genre of the text? Is there anything in terms of meaning, relations and cohesion that you find interesting? As always, try to place your observations within an analysis of interpretative effects.

2.5 Structure

2.5.1 The linguistic rank scale

In this section, we'll focus on grammar. Generally grammar can be the study of either morphology or syntax.

KEY TERMS

Morphology: the study of word formation

Syntax: the study of how words form larger structures such as phrases, clauses and sentences

---

It's first worth highlighting the relationship between different structural units of language. The linguistic rank scale (Figure 2.2) helps to do this. Moving from left to right along the scale, you can see how smaller units combine to form larger meaningful structures.

Figure 2.2: The linguistic rank scale

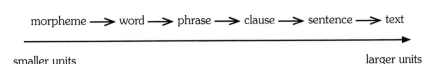

morpheme ⟶ word ⟶ phrase ⟶ clause ⟶ sentence ⟶ text

smaller units   larger units

The smallest unit is the morpheme, from which words are formed. Usually a word will consist of at least a root morpheme, and often a root morpheme plus an affix. For example, the noun *appointment* has a root *appoint* and an ending affix, or suffix, *-ment*. The noun *disappointment* is formed by the addition of a further initial affix, or prefix, *dis-*.

Together affixes either have an inflectional function to show plural nouns (*gate* + *-s* = *gates*) or a shift in verb tense (e.g. *walk* + *-ed* = *walked*), or a derivational function, for example to form a new word by being added to a root (as in the *appointment/disappointment* examples above).

KEY TERMS

Root morpheme: a morpheme that can stand on its own and can usually form a word in its own right

Affix: the generic term for an addition to a root (a prefix or suffix) which modifies its meaning or creates a new word

Suffix: a morpheme that comes after a root word to modify its meaning

Prefix: a morpheme that goes before a root word to modify its meaning

Inflectional function: the way that an affix shows a grammatical category such as a verb tense or a plural noun

Derivational function: the way that an affix helps form a new word by attaching itself to a root

---

2.5.2 Phrases

Looking at the linguistic rank scale (Figure 2.2) you can see that a phrase is a structure that sits at a level between a word and a clause. It is centred around a head word. Key phrase types include:

- noun phrase

- verb phrase

- adjective phrase

- adverb phrase

- prepositional phrase.

In the extract from *The Small Hand* (Text 2F), 'a large, overgrown, empty, abandoned garden' is an example of a noun phrase. It contains a head word 'garden' and a determiner 'a', as well as four adjectives positioned before the noun, which act as pre-modifiers. In the context of this extract, the narrator's choice to use a heavily pre-modified noun phrase is in itself significant: the use of pre-modification adds a precision and a richness to the scene being described that would be unavailable if a simple determiner + noun structure had been used, or even if one or two adjectives had been used. This noun phrase's constituent elements can be labelled as follows:

d m   m   m   m   h

a large, overgrown, empty, abandoned garden

Key

Head word (h)

Determiner (d)

Modifier (m)

Other types of phrase are named after their head words. A verb phrase is centred around a main verb which acts as the head word. In addition, a verb phrase may also include an auxiliary verb to show either tense (the primary auxiliary verbs *be*, *do* and *have*) or a degree of commitment towards an event or person (the modal auxiliary verbs such as *may*, *could*, *must*). An adjective phrase has an adjective as its head word and an adverb phrase an adverb as its head word. Adjective and adverb phrases can be modified in a similar way to noun phrases or can simply be single words. For example:

- **Verb phrase:** *am going* (primary auxiliary verb + head word), *might go* (modal auxiliary verb + head word), *went* (head word)

- **Adjective phrase:** *quite big* (modifying adverb + head word), *happy* (head word)

- **Adverb phrase:** *very quickly* (modifying adverb + head word), *probably* (head word)

Finally prepositional phrases are headed by prepositions, which show spatial relationships. Sometimes prepositional phrases can post-modify or qualify noun phrases such as in 'the large house by the sea', where 'by the sea' is a prepositional phrase containing a preposition as head word and an embedded noun phrase 'the sea'. The potential for prepositional phrases to be recursive can yield some interesting stylistic effects. For example, look at Text 2G, an extract from *Funnybones*, a book for young readers.

KEY TERMS

Noun phrase: a group of words that has a noun as its head word

Head word: the main word in the phrase

Pre-modifier: a word that goes before the head noun to add detail or clarify some aspect of it

Verb phrase: a group of words that has a verb as its head word

Primary auxiliary verb: an auxiliary verb that joins with a main verb to show tense

Modal auxiliary verb: an auxiliary verb that joins with a main verb to show the degree of commitment towards an event or person that a speaker holds

Adjective phrase: a group of words that has an adjective as its head word

Adverb phrase: a group of words that has an adverb as its head word

Prepositional phrase: a group of words that has a preposition as its head word

Text 2G

This is how the story begins.

On a dark dark hill

there was a dark dark town.

In the dark dark town

there was a dark dark street.

In the dark dark street

there was a dark dark house.

In the dark dark house

there was a dark dark staircase.

Down the dark dark staircase

there was a dark dark cellar.

And in the dark dark cellar...

...some skeletons lived.

Extract from *Funnybones*, Janet Ahlberg and Alan Ahlberg, Puffin (1999)

In this extract, the pattern of prepositional phrases (e.g. 'on a dark dark hill') followed by 'there was a' plus a new noun phrase construction (e.g. 'there was a dark dark street') guides the reader through the text. Each new noun phrase becomes embedded in the following prepositional phrase to create a pattern that gradually zooms in from the 'dark dark hill' to the 'dark dark cellar'. The repeated multiple pre-modification using the adjective 'dark' is designed to create a sense of mystery and suspense for its young audience, leading to the revelation that some skeletons live in the cellar!

2.5.3 Clauses and sentences

Phrases can form larger structures called clauses, which have constituent elements. Table 2.2 shows how these constituent elements operate.

KEY TERM

Constituent elements: the particular parts of a phrase or clause

Table 2.2: Constituent elements of the clause

Constituent element	Description
Subject (S): usually a noun phrase	Acts as the key focus of the clause
Verb (V): a verb phrase	Provides the information about the process at the centre of the clause
Object (O): usually a noun phrase	Identifies the entity being acted on by the action of a verb process
Complement (C): usually a noun phrase or adjective phrase	The attribute or identifying aspect of a subject in a relational verb process
Adverbial (A): usually an adverb or prepositional phrase	Identifies the circumstances of a verb process in terms of time, place or manner

Looking back at some of the literary examples in this chapter, the following clause patterns can be found.

S   V
I pushed (*The Small Hand*)

S   V   O
I touched (the cold iron latch) (*The Small Hand*)

      S   V   C

There was (a dark dark house) (*Funnybones*)

      S   V   O   A

I (was peeling) (the potatoes) (for our tea) ('Night after night')

Clauses can also form larger multi-clause structures. Coordinate clauses are introduced by one of the coordinating conjunctions *and*, *but*, *or* and are independent in so far as they can stand on their own and make complete sense. In contrast, a subordinate clause is introduced by a subordinating conjunction, such as *although*, *because*, and depends on a main clause to give a fully formed structure that makes sense. Sometimes, however, clauses are verbless. This is in itself a form of foregrounding since a verbless clause (also called a minor sentence) grammatically deviates from the conventional structure of a clause. A verbless clause is often used for striking or dramatic effects.

KEY TERMS

Coordinate clause: a clause that is introduced by one of the coordinating conjunctions

Subordinate clause: a clause that is introduced by a subordinating conjunction and depends on a main clause to give a complete sense of meaning

Main clause: a unit in a multi-clause structure that can stand on its own and make complete sense

Verbless clause: a clause that does not contain a verb

You can see examples of all of these clause types in Text 2H, an extract from 'Dead on the hour', a short story by Peter James. In this story the main character, Sandra, is a carer for her elderly mother. In this extract, Sandra has just discovered that her mother has died.

Text 2H

She dozed fitfully, listening for the chimes of the grandfather clock, but heard only the rising, then abating dawn chorus. Finally, she got out of bed, pulled on her dressing gown, closed the door and stood for a moment on the landing. Bitumen-black shadows rose out of the darkness to enfold her. She stared at the door of her mother's room and felt a tightness grip her throat. Normally she would have been able to hear the clock ticking, but it was silent. Puzzled, she went downstairs into the hall. The hands of the grandfather clock pointed to three o'clock. It had stopped, she realised, her eyes sliding to her own wristwatch. It was six forty-five.

Then she felt a deep unease. Three o'clock. She remembered now; it was coming back. She remembered what grief had made her forget earlier. Three o'clock. She glanced at her watch to imprint it on her mind. Information the doctor might want to know: her mother had died at three o'clock precisely.

Extract from 'Dead on the hour', Peter James, Macmillan (2014)

The extract contains a number of different clause types, as shown below. In multi-clause structures, each clause is placed in between * *.

- **Single clause:** 'It was six forty-five.'

- **Coordinate clauses:** 'Finally, *she got out of bed*, and *pulled on her dressing gown*, and *closed the door* and *stood for a moment on the landing.*'

- **Main clause + subordinate clause:** '*Bitumen-black shadows rose out of the darkness* *to enfold her.*'

- **Verbless clause:** 'Three o'clock.'

2.5.4 Active and passive voice

Read Text 21, taken from Emma Healey's novel *Elizabeth is Missing*. The narrator is recounting meeting a fellow resident in an elderly people's home.

Text 21

I take the flower and close my fist around it as she pulls the whole bunch of plastic stems from the vase and thrusts them at me.

Extract from *Elizabeth is Missing*, Emma Healey, Penguin (2014)

This extract contains the following clauses and elements:

I take the flower (SVO)

I close my fist around it (SVOA)

she pulls the whole bunch of plastic stems from the vase (SVOA)

she thrusts them at me (SVOA)

In each clause, the entity responsible for carrying out the verb (the agent) is placed in the subject position. Configuring the clause in this way is effectively like shining a spotlight on the agent to draw attention to its importance. Or, in other words, using the active voice foregrounds the agent of a clause.

However, example 1 could be rewritten as follows:

The flower was taken by me

In this instance, the passive voice involves moving the entity directly acted on by the verb (the patient) to the subject position in the clause with the agent positioned at end of the clause. In this case, prominence is given to the flower and the agent is defocused. Grammatically, the passive voice is formed by changing the verb phrase to a form of *to be* + participle form (verb root + *-en/-ed*) and shifting the agent to the end of the clause within a prepositional phrase.

KEY TERMS

Agent: the entity responsible for carrying out the verb in an action process

Active voice: a clause structure where the agent is placed in subject position for prominence

Passive voice: a clause structure where the patient is the subject and the agent is omitted or placed later on using a prepositional phrase

Patient: the entity directly acted on by the verb in an action process

In fact, passive constructions may omit the agent entirely. This can have the effect of placing even more emphasis on the entity affected by the verb and/or avoiding drawing attention to the person or group responsible for the action. For example:

The flower was taken

Finally, there are some other ways that active and passive constructions may be used within larger constructions to foreground or marginalise certain key aspects. For example, look at the following ways that example 1 could have been presented:

Reported form: agency subordinated and delayed in active voice

Example: I/s(he) said I took the flower

Reported form: agency defocused in passive voice

Example: I/s(he) said the flower was taken by me

Reported form: agency removed in passive voice

Example: I/s(he) said the flower was taken

Nominalised form: verb process reified (shifted to form the noun phrase 'The taking')

Example: The taking of the flower

ACTIVITY 2.3

Looking at clausal patterns

Look at Text 2J, taken from Ian McEwan's novel *The Children Act*. In this extract, the narrator is reflecting on her husband's decision to return to her following an affair.

Identify the different types of clause in this extract and comment on any patterns you can see.

Text 2J

> She stopped by the kitchen to take an apple and a banana from the shopping on the table. Having them in her hand as she went towards the bedroom brought back her relatively happy walk home from work. She had felt the beginnings of some ease. Hard to recapture now. She pushed open the door and saw his suitcase standing upright and prim on the wheels by the bed. Then it came to her plainly what she felt about Jack's return. So simple. It was disappointment that he had not stayed away. Just a little longer. Nothing more than that. Disappointment.
>
> Extract from *The Children Act*, Ian McEwan, Random House (2014)

2.6 Sounds

The study of sounds involves examining the areas of both phonetics and phonology. As with single words and larger structures, in this section you will look at how patterns in sounds can lead to rich interpretative effects.

KEY TERMS

Phonetics: the area of study that is concerned with investigating how sounds are actually produced by language users

Phonology: the area of study that refers to the more abstract sound system

2.6.1 Describing sounds

The international phonetic alphabet (IPA) offers a way of categorising phonemes so as to examine any patterns in the sound system that might have interpretative significance. Table 2.3 shows the IPA symbols. The underlined part of each example word corresponds to a symbol, but note that this is how the word would be pronounced in Received Pronunciation (RP); for example the vowel in the word 'bath' is pronounced as /ɑː/ in RP but in many parts of the UK as /æ/.

> **KEY TERMS**
>
> **International phonetic alphabet (IPA):** a system for showing the different sounds possible
>
> **Phoneme:** the smallest meaningful distinct unit in the sound system

Table 2.3: Consonants and vowels

Consonants		Vowels	
p	pip	**Short vowels**	
b	bib	ɪ	pit
t	ten	e	pet
d	den	æ	pat
k	cat	ɒ	pot
g	get	ʌ	but
f	fish	ʊ	book
v	voice	ə	mother
θ	thigh	**Long vowels**	
ð	this	iː	bean
s	set	ɜː	burn
z	zoo	ɑː	barn
ʃ	ship	ɔː	born
ʒ	measure	uː	boon
h	hen	**Diphthongs**	
tʃ	church	aɪ	bite
dʒ	judge	eɪ	bait
m	man	ɔɪ	boy

Consonants		Vowels	
n	now	əʊ	toe
ŋ	sing	aʊ	house
l	let	ʊə	cure
r	ride	ɪə	ear
w	wet	eə	air
j	yet		

2.6.2 Sound groups

As Table 2.3 shows, vowels can be grouped depending on whether they are short, long or diphthongs.

Consonant sounds can be grouped in terms of how they are articulated in the mouth. All consonant sounds involve the restriction of airflow by articulators in the vocal tract: either the lips coming together (labial), or the tongue being positioned against the teeth (dental) or in some part of the roof of the mouth (alveolar ridge, hard and soft palate). These articulators are shown in Figure 2.3.

Figure 2.3: Articulators

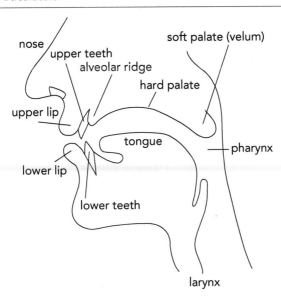

Consonant sounds can be categorised as shown in Table 2.4.

Table 2.4: Consonant groups

Consonant group	Description	Members
Plosive	Produced by the articulators coming together to stop the airflow and then being released	p, b (labial) t, d (alveolar) k, g (soft palate)
Fricative	Produced by the articulators being positioned together but a small gap remaining through which the sound comes	θ, ð (dental) f, v (labio-dental: lower lip against upper teeth) s, z (alveolar) ʃ, ʒ (post alveolar)
Affricate	Produced by the articulators coming together, then released but in a way that is similar to the friction sound of a fricative	dʒ, tʃ (hard palate)
Nasal	Produced by articulators stopping the airflow with a release through the nose	m (labial) n (alveolar) ŋ (soft palate)
Lateral	Produced by articulators coming together and air being released over the sides of the tongue	l (alveolar)
Approximant	Produced in a similar way to other consonant sounds but without the articulators fully coming together	w (labial) r (alveolar) j (hard palate)

2.6.3 Sound iconicity

Literary texts often have foregrounded sound patterns that mirror the actions they describe, or which are intended to draw attention to some relationship between sound and form. This is known as sound iconicity. However, it's important to remember that sounds in themselves do not have inherent meaning. It is only ever feasible to look at the wider context in which a sound appears and think about the possible symbolic value that the sound might have. For example, there's no justification for arguing that /s/ has an inherent sliding quality to it, but in Text 2K, an extract from William Wordsworth's *The Prelude*, we can say that in the context of the extract about skating the repeated /s/ pattern has the effect of heightening the experience for a reader in imagining the sound of the skaters moving across the ice. Of course, this can only happen if a reader is aware of the sound that a skater on ice makes and can consequently see /s/ as having symbolic value.

> KEY TERM
>
> **Sound iconicity:** the matching of sound to an aspect of meaning

Text 2K

All shod with steel,

We hissed across the polished ice

> Extract from 'The Prelude', William Wordsworth (1850)

Read Text 2L, the first four lines of Walter de La Mare's (1912) poem 'The Listeners'.

Text 2L

'Is there anybody there?' said the Traveller,

Knocking on the moonlight door;

And his horse in the silence champed the grasses

Of the forest's ferny floor

> Extract from 'The Listeners', Walter de la Mare (1912)

In this extract, de la Mare uses sound as follows:

- In line 2, the repetition of the plosive sounds /k/ and /d/ heighten the sense of the traveller knocking on the door. A set of consonant sounds repeated for effect is also known as consonance.

- Equally, in line 2, the repeated short vowel sound/ɒ/ in 'knocking' and 'on' is an example of assonance. This pattern combines with the long vowel /u:/ and the diphthong /ʊə/ to enhance the rhythmic sense of the knocking.

- In line 3, the fricative and affricate sounds /s/ and /tʃ/ mimic the eerie silence of the location, the foregrounded pattern of fricatives being broken by the affricate /tʃ/ to represent the sound of the horse eating. This use is also known as sibilance.

- In line 4, a further pattern of fricative /f/ sounds and a replication of the short vowel–long vowel–diphthong pattern of line 2 in /ɒ/, /ə/, /ɒ/, /e/, /ɜ:/, /i:/, /ʊə/ emphasise both the environment and the rhythm of the horse eating.

KEY TERMS

Consonance: a pattern of repeated consonant sounds for effect

Assonance: a pattern of repeated vowel sounds for effect

Sibilance: a pattern of repeated fricative sounds for effect

ACTIVITY 2.4

Exploring sounds in poetry

Read Text 2M, 'Anthem for Doomed Youth', written in 1917 by the English First World War poet Wilfred Owen. Identify any significant sound patterns and comment on their effect on you as a reader.

Text 2M

What passing-bells for these who die as cattle?

— Only the monstrous anger of the guns.

Only the stuttering rifles' rapid rattle

Can patter out their hasty orisons.

No mockeries now for them; no prayers nor bells;

Nor any voice of mourning save the choirs,—

The shrill, demented choirs of wailing shells;

And bugles calling for them from sad shires.

What candles may be held to speed them all?

Not in the hands of boys, but in their eyes

Shall shine the holy glimmers of goodbyes.

The pallor of girls' brows shall be their pall;

Their flowers the tenderness of patient minds,

And each slow dusk a drawing-down of blinds.

'Anthem for Doomed Youth', Wilfred Owen (1917)

2.7 Developing writing as a response

In this final section, you will look at how you can ensure that your writing remains tight and focused when analysing literary texts.

It's important, of course, to remember the key principles of stylistics that were discussed in the opening chapter. These included the fact that stylistics promotes using clearly defined metalanguage to ensure that all the stages of any analysis are open to scrutiny by other researchers in the field. Chapter 1 emphasised the three Rs as proposed by Simpson (2014):

- Stylistic analysis should be rigorous.

- Stylistic analysis should be retrievable.

- Stylistic analysis should be replicable.

Following these principles, doing work in stylistics means that your writing needs to be:

- systematic and clear

- focused both on identifying language *and* providing an interpretation at all times

- accountable to the text itself.

Read Text 2N, an extract from the nineteenth-century novel *Great Expectations* by Charles Dickens. This extract occurs at the beginning of the novel and is narrated by the main character Pip.

Text 2N

Ours was the marsh country, down by the river, within, as the river wound, twenty miles from the sea. My first most vivid and broad impression of the identity of things, seems to me to have been gained on a memorable raw afternoon towards evening. At such a time I found out for certain, that this bleak place overgrown with nettles was the churchyard; and that Philip Pirrip, late of this parish, and also Georgiana wife of the above, were dead and buried; and that Alexander, Bartholomew, Abraham, Tobias, and Roger, infant children of the aforesaid, were also dead and buried; and that the dark flat wilderness beyond the churchyard, intersected with dykes and mounds and gates, with scattered cattle feeding on it, was the marshes; and that the low leaden line beyond, was the river; and that the distant savage lair from which the wind was rushing, was the sea; and that the small bundle of shivers growing afraid of it all and beginning to cry, was Pip.

Extract from *Great Expectations*, Charles Dickens (1861)

Here are the openings to three student responses to the extract.

Student response 1

In this extract, Dickens presents a terrifying scene. The narrator is scared, shown through the use of negative words. He creates a barren scene to affect the reader.

Student response 2

Dickens moves across the narrative landscape with the ease and skill of a master. His deft hand paints a subtly worrying portrait of the wilderness of the marshes, grounded in Pip's family history, which perpetually haunts the retrospective but now disembodied narrator. The cries of individual words reverberate across the page and across time; the bleakness stands guard-like over any attempt to reclaim the narrative self.

Student response 3

In this extract, there is heavy use of pre-modification in noun phrases. There is a clear SVC pattern where the subject is a heavily modified noun phrase with further embedded adjective and prepositional phrases and the complement a straightforward determiner + head noun construction, for example 'this bleak place overgrown with nettles was the churchyard'. This pattern is repeated a further four times across the remaining clauses in the extract.

There are problems with the approach taken in each response. In the first response, the comments are simply hunches, offering some tentative ideas but doing so in a vague and impressionistic way. The use of terms such as 'negative words' and 'affects the reader' mean very little and simply fill out the 'analysis'.

The second response is also problematic. Here, there is an over-reliance on rhetoric, complex ideas and elevated, grand-sounding words. The style is dense and it's difficult to work out exactly what is meant by comments like 'The cries of individual words reverberate across the page'. (You can test this out by asking different people what this might mean; you will probably receive very different answers.) The writing relies on its own rhetorical flourishes and consequently it's difficult to engage with the ideas since they are not grounded in an analysis of the language of the text itself. In many ways, this is the worst kind of literary criticism.

Finally, the third response does engage with language, carefully highlighting some foregrounded features and commenting on what is clearly an important textual pattern. However, there is no interpretative comment whatsoever and consequently the text becomes simply a vehicle for demonstrating whatever language features the student has learnt. The response thus shows evidence of linguistic knowledge but is not good stylistics.

If you are beginning to develop your own skills in analysing texts, there are two ways of planning and shaping your thoughts and writing so as to avoid the types of response shown above. The first way is to start with your initial thoughts on the text, jotting down some ideas on themes, mood and character. Then, for each of ideas, try to isolate some specific language feature or pattern located in the text that you feel supports this interpretation or idea. You can then ensure that you give these features coverage in your writing so that your analysis is accountable to the text.

The second way is to start with a specific language feature or pattern. Once you have spotted something you feel is important, aim to ask:

- Why is this feature or pattern here?

- What is the interpretative effect on me as a reader?

- How significant is this in relation to other parts of the text?

By asking these questions, you should ensure that your writing is interpretative instead of merely demonstrating knowledge of linguistics.

ACTIVITY 2.5

Rewriting to improve

Using what you have learnt in this chapter, rewrite one of the three student responses so as to transform it into a piece of stylistic analysis. Remember that you need to supply a close linguistic analysis and an interpretation, and that the source of the interpretation should be the linguistic features of the text itself.

PRACTICE QUESTION

Stylistic analysis of 'Poem'

Read Text 20, 'Poem', by Simon Armitage. Complete a close stylistic analysis of this poem using the toolkit you have explored in this chapter. Ensure that you keep a tight focus on language and have provided an interpretation of the effects of language choices. You could start by using either one of the two 'ways in' to a text discussed above.

Text 20

And if it snowed and snow covered the drive
he took a spade and tossed it to one side.
And always tucked his daughter up at night
And slippered her the one time that she lied.

And every week he tipped up half his wage.
And what he didn't spend each week he saved.
And praised his wife for every meal she made.
And once, for laughing, punched her in the face.

And for his mum he hired a private nurse.
And every Sunday taxied her to church.
And he blubbed when she went from bad to worse.
And twice he lifted ten quid from her purse.

Here's how they rated him when they looked back:
sometimes he did this, sometimes he did that.

'Poem', Simon Armitage (1992)

RESEARCH QUESTION

Comparing literary and non-literary texts

You could examine the characteristics of literary texts in more detail by collecting some examples of non-literary material that rely on foregrounding. Compare this with a literary extract that you feel relies on foregrounding to achieve its effects. What similarities and differences do you notice between the ways that foregrounding operates in these texts? Does this say anything to you about what makes a text 'literary'?

Wider reading

You can find out more about the topics in this chapter by reading the following:

Russian formalism

Cook, G. (1994) *Discourse and Literature*. Oxford: Oxford University Press.

Foregrounding theory

Leech, G. (2008) *Language in Literature: Style and Foregrounding*. London: Pearson.

Parallelism and deviation

Leech, G. and Short, M. (2007) *Style in Fiction: A Linguistic Introduction to English Fictional Prose* (Second edition). London: Longman.

Methods and tools for stylistics

Gregoriou, C. (2008) *English Literary Stylistics*. Basingstoke: Palgrave Macmillan.

Mullany, L. and Stockwell, P. (2015) *Introducing English Language: A Resource Book for Students* (Second edition). London: Routledge.

Simpson, P. (2014) *Stylistics: A Resource Book for Students* (Second edition). London: Routledge.

Stockwell, P. (2002) *Cognitive Poetics: An Introduction*. London: Routledge.

Toolan, M. (1998) *Language in Literature: An Introduction to Stylistics*. London: Hodder.

Chapter 3
Doing stylistics

In this chapter you will:

- Explore some further concepts and methods that will enable you to undertake a stylistic analysis of any literary text

- Develop your toolkit to include ways of analysing speech and thought, attitude and point of view, and the presentation of characters and events across the three genres of literary fiction

3.1 Introduction

This chapter is designed to build on Chapter 2 by offering you more detailed models and methods of analysis to support your work with literary texts. Each section outlines a different area of language study and explains how this may be useful in undertaking work in stylistics.

3.2 Speech and thought presentation

3.2.1 Categories of speech and thought

Although there are some differences between naturally occurring speech and literary representations of spoken language, these are not as far-reaching as might be thought. Indeed corpus studies that use computer software to analyse large sets of data show that aside from features such as pauses and fillers (words like 'er' and 'um'), literary speech has many of the same characteristics as its real-life counterpart. In this section, you will explore the possible ways that authors may present speech, focusing on the degree to which that speech is presented directly or mediated in some way through a narrating voice.

As an example, look at Text 3A, which is an extract from Shirley Jackson's *We Have Always Lived in the Castle*. There are three examples of speech presentation here, numbered in brackets.

Text 3A

'I have the newspaper clippings,' Uncle Julian said uncertainly (1). 'I have my notes,' he told Helen Clarke (2), 'I have written everything down' (3).

Extract from *We Have Always Lived in the Castle*,
Shirley Jackson, Viking Press (1962)

This extract contains three examples where the character, Uncle Julian, is talking. The first two consist of what is known as Direct Speech (DS). In these examples, Uncle Julian's words, part of an overall third-person narration, are presented in speech marks to show that they are the exact words spoken by him and are followed by a reporting clause. This means the reader gets a faithful representation of Uncle Julian's words, although in the first example, the modifying of the speech verb 'said' with the adverb 'uncertainly' filters the words to some degree through the narrating voice (it is the narrator who is responsible for telling the reader how Uncle Julian spoke). In the second reporting clause, however, 'he told Helen Clarke' is more neutral. In the third example, Uncle Julian's words, 'I have written everything down', are not framed by a reporting clause. Its complete freedom from any narrator mediation accounts for the fact that this is known as Free Direct Speech (FDS).

KEY TERMS

Direct Speech/Thought: speech or thought that is presented word for word but with a speech/thought clause added by the narrator

Free Direct Speech/Thought: speech or thought that is presented word for word with no speech/thought clause added by the narrator

---

Direct Speech and Free Direct Speech are only two possible ways that authors might choose to represent speech. Four further ways, based on the extract from *We Have Always Lived in the Castle*, are as follows:

Indirect Speech (IS)

Example: Uncle Julian said that he had the newspaper clippings and his notes, and that he had written everything down.

In this example of Indirect Speech (IS), most of what Uncle Julian said is retained but the use of the third-person pronoun 'he' and the possessive determiner 'his' reconfigures the words from the narrator's perspective. In addition, the removal of the speech marks makes the speech itself part of an embedded subordinate clause dependent on the main reporting clause. And the tense is backshifted (demonstrated in the change from 'have' to 'had') so as to present the words spoken within the time frame of the narrating voice rather than Uncle Julian's.

KEY TERM

Indirect Speech/Thought: speech or thought that is framed by the narrator but retains an element of what was said by the character

---

Free Indirect Speech (FIS)

Example: He has the newspaper clippings and his notes and has written everything down.

In this example of Free Indirect Speech (FIS), there is no reporting clause and the tense remains as it is in Direct Speech. The effect is that the words seem both framed by the narrator but also closer to Uncle Julian's perspective than in Indirect Speech.

Narrator's Representation of Speech Act (NRSA)

Example: Uncle Julian spoke about his possessions.

In this example of Narrator's Representation of Speech Act (NRSA), Uncle Julian's words have been summarised. The reader is provided with some indication of what was said, but the narrator does not reveal the actual words to us.

Narrator's Representation of Speech (NRS)

Example: Uncle Julian spoke to us.

In this instance of Narrator's Representation of Speech (NRS), only the fact that Uncle Julian spoke is relayed to the reader; any indication of what was said is omitted.

We can place these categories of speech along a continuum, as on Figure 3.1, to show how each provides a distinctive way of representing a character's words.

Figure 3.1: Continuum of speech presentation

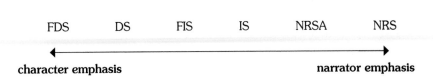

| FDS | DS | FIS | IS | NRSA | NRS |

character emphasis   **narrator emphasis**

The Language of Literature: An Introduction to Stylistics

Moving from left to right along the continuum results in an increase in the framing of a character's words by the narrative voice. At one extreme end (Narrator's Representation of Speech Act and Narrator's Representation of Speech), the perceived interference by a narrator is so great that it can be difficult to work out exactly what a character said. This may cause the reader to question a character's (or indeed the narrator's) reliability. Towards the middle, Free Indirect Speech integrates both a narrator's and a character's perspective and so is often thought of as a halfway mode, revealing two different yet integrated points of view. At the other extreme, Free Direct Speech and Direct Speech forms provide largely unmediated character speech. One effect of this may be to give the reader a closer insight into a character's thought processes and provide a more realistic portrayal of speech and dialogue. However, long stretches of (particularly) Free Direct Speech may give a narrative a free-flowing yet confusing feel given that there is no support from the narrator in shaping dialogue. For example, in Text 3B, taken from Christos Tsiolkas' *The Slap*, the reader has to work hard to keep track of which character is talking.

Text 3B

She rang Aisha as soon as she walked into her apartment.

'Are you free tomorrow?'

'Thursday is a bad day. I'm working till eight.'

'Friday?'

'What's this about?'

'I need some advice.'

'Rhys?'

'Friday?'

Extract from *The Slap*, Christos Tsiolkas, Allen & Unwin (2008)

These speech categories can also be used to explain and explore the different options for presenting characters' thoughts. Moving from a character to a narrator emphasis we have Free Direct Thought (FDT), Direct Thought (DT), Free Indirect Thought (FIT), Indirect Thought (IT), Narrator's Representation of Thought Act (NRTA) and Narrator's Representation of Thought (NRT). These modes of thought presentation have largely the same effect as speech presentation in terms of how they provide degrees of character or narrator emphasis.

ACTIVITY 3.1

Exploring speech and thought presentation

You can explore the effects of some of the patterns discussed above in extracts of your own choice. For a more subtle exploration of how speech and thought presentation can operate, read Text 3C, the opening of 'In winter the sky', a short story by Jon McGregor. What do you notice about the ways that speech and thought are presented here? What effect does this have on you as a reader?

Text 3C

He had something to tell her. He announced this the next day. After the fog had cleared, while the floods still lay over the fields. It looked like a difficult thing for him to say. His hands were shaking. She asked him if it couldn't wait until after she'd done some work, and he said that there was always something else to do, some other reason to wait and not to talk. All right, she said. Fine, bring the dogs. They gave his father some lunch, and they walked out together along the path beside the drainage canal.

She knew what he wanted to tell her, but she didn't know what he would say.

Extract from 'In winter the sky', Jon McGregor, Bloomsbury (2012)

Another really interesting context in which to think about speech and thought presentation is in plays and on the screen. Let's start with plays.

3.2.2 Speech and thought in drama

The opportunities afforded to playwrights to render speech and thought are very different to those of authors. As plays are predominantly constituted of dialogue, Free Direct Speech is the primary form of speech presentation available. A good example of this is Text 3D, an extract from Samuel Beckett's absurdist drama *Waiting for Godot*.

Text 3D

ESTRAGON:	What's the matter with you all?
VLADIMIR:	Help!
ESTRAGON:	I'm going.
VLADIMIR:	Don't leave me! They'll kill me!
POZZO:	Where am I?

VLADIMIR:	Gogo!
POZZO:	Help!
VLADIMIR:	Help!
ESTRAGON:	I'm going.
VLADIMIR:	Help me up first. Then we'll go together.
ESTRAGON:	You promise?
VLADIMIR:	I swear it!
ESTRAGON:	And we'll never come back?
VLADIMIR:	Never!

Extract from *Waiting for Godot*, Samuel Beckett,
Les Editions de Minuit (1953)

This example highlights a crucial point about the stylistic analysis of plays, which needs to be addressed before moving forward to anything else: analysing a play script and analysing a performance of that play are two very different tasks. Here, for instance, you see only Beckett's script. In the intervening years since the play was written it has been performed countless times and rendered and reinterpreted by each director and cast in lots and lots of different ways. The difference between analysing a script and a performance largely arises from the stylistic feature currently being discussed: the script is comprised largely of Free Direct Speech, and nothing else. This means that the 'text' will be different from performance to performance, possibly even from night to night of the same company's performance, because there is so much stylistic detail not defined by the written text.

For instance, an analysis of the speech presented here enables you to infer intonation through the punctuation. You could interpret the question mark concluding Estragon's 'And we'll never come back?' and the exclamation mark concluding Vladimir's 'Never!' as the virtual equivalents of reporting clauses. That is, if the text were a novel, you might expect it to read:

'And we'll never come back?' Estragon asked.

'Never!' Vladimir exclaimed.

However, you have no way to know whether this punctuation is heeded in any given performance. Similarly you might expect that features of spoken discourse that are difficult to render in written forms might be present in a performance, such as interruptions, false starts and fillers, either deliberately or by accident.

There are limited opportunities for playwrights to engage in any thought presentation at all. There are two main techniques playwrights use to get around this issue. First, there is the possibility of attempting to influence performances via the use of stage directions. This can offer some presentation of character thought, likely in the form of Narrator's Representation of Thought or possibly Narrator's Representation of Thought Acts, with the playwright functioning in the role of narrator. George Bernard Shaw, for example, has a tendency to offer long and very detailed stage directions. You can see an example of this shifting into thought presentation in various directions throughout his play *Mrs Warren's Profession*. For example, read Text 3E and Text 3F.

Text 3E

VIVIE: *<not at all pleased>* Did she? Hm! My mother has rather a trick of taking me by surprise – to see how I behave myself when she's away, I suppose. I fancy I shall take my mother very much by surprise one of these days. I fancy I shall if she makes arrangements that concern me without consulting me beforehand. She hasn't come.

PRAED: *<embarrassed>* I'm really very sorry.

VIVIE: *<throwing off her displeasure>* It's not your fault, Mr Praed, is it? And I'm very glad you've come. You are the only one of my mother's friends I have ever asked her to bring to see me.

PRAED: *<relieved and delighted>* Oh, now this is really very good of you Miss Warren!

Extract from *Mrs Warren's Profession*, Act I,
George Bernard Shaw (1893)

Text 3F

Mrs Warren, silenced for a moment, looks forlornly at Vivie, who waits, secretly hoping that the combat is over.

Extract from *Mrs Warren's Profession*, Act V,
George Bernard Shaw (1893)

Text 3E offers a series of italicised comments preceding the Free Direct Speech, which arguably offer some Narrator's Representation of Thought. The reader is not given any indication of the specific thoughts flowing through Vivie's mind but, for example, they are told that her thoughts can be initially characterised as displeasure which she then subsequently 'throws off'. In Text 3F, something closer to a Narrator's Representation of Thought Act is evident: the phrase 'secretly hoping that the combat is over' offers a more concrete indication of what Vivie thought, but without any clear sense of what she thought specifically.

In both cases the thought presentation forms part of the written text, and thus could be stylistically analysed as such, but this presentation will not manifest in a performance of Shaw's play, except through the behaviour of the actors. As such, this kind of thought presentation offers a fascinating basis for comparative stylistic analysis between the written version of a play and a particular performance of it.

The second technique offers playwrights a way to incorporate Free Direct Thought presentation in drama: the use of the monologues and asides. Here, characters figuratively step out of a scene and speak directly to the audience, sharing their thoughts through this metaphorical window into their mind. Perhaps the most famous play that utilises this technique is Shakespeare's *Henry V*. You can see this technique used following Henry's rousing St Crispin's Day speech where he enthuses his troops with visions of victory and then defiantly turns away Montjoy, the French Herald, who has come to offer terms of surrender. In Text 3G you can see Free Direct Thought offered in the form of an aside used to reveal a sharp contrast, exacerbated by the juxtaposition of what Henry says – in his Direct Speech – and what he is actually thinking.

Text 3G

KING: Come thou no more for ransom, gentle herald.

     They shall have none, I swear, but these my joints,

     Which if they have, as I will leave 'em them,

     Shall yield them little. Tell the Constable.

MONTJOY: I shall, King Harry. And so fare thee well.

     Thou never shalt hear herald any more. *Exit.*

KING: *<Aside>* I fear thou wilt once more come again for a ransom.

     Extract from *Henry V*, Act IV, Scene iii, William Shakespeare

---

Such instances of Free Direct Thought will be common to both written play texts and their corresponding performances, though again the way in which such lines are uttered in various productions has the potential to create distinct stylistic effects.

A final technique one might consider as a way in which to insert some insight into characters' thoughts into dramatic texts is the use of modality in Direct Speech, where characters share their thoughts with other characters using phrases such as 'I think', 'I feel', 'I want', 'I wish', and so on. How exactly to classify such utterances is open to debate, though perhaps they might best be thought of as instances of Direct Thought embedded within Direct Speech.

3.2.3 Speech and thought on screen

A similar challenge of representing thought is posed by the medium of screen drama, whether film or television. As with plays, writers often rely on actors' body language, facial expressions and intonation to help viewers infer thought processes. Another technique often utilised is the voiceover, where a character will share their thoughts with the audience whilst a scene continues to play, indicating that this is something that only the viewer, and not the other characters, can hear.

ACTIVITY 3.2

Thought presentation on screen

Choose a scene from a television programme or film that you like. Can you detect any thought presentation? If so, how has this been achieved? If not, what is the effect of its absence? How might the scene be different if you had access to the characters' thoughts?

3.3 Modality

A character or a narrator's attitude towards events and other characters can be demonstrated in a number of different ways, for example by their actions and the ways in which they speak and think. One specific way in which attitudes are framed is through the use of modal expressions. In linguistics, modality is the umbrella term used to describe language that presents an individual's opinion of or commitment to any state of affairs. In Chapter 2, you saw that modal auxiliary verbs often combine with main verbs to emphasise some level of certainty or necessity. In addition to auxiliary verbs, modality is also often realised in other linguistic forms, such as:

- modal lexical verbs (e.g. *like, hope, believe*)

- modal adjectives (e.g. *sure, certain, doubtful*)

- modal adverbs (e.g. *perhaps, possibly, maybe*)

- modal tags (e.g. *I guess*).

KEY TERM

Modality: the term used to describe language that presents degrees of attitude or commitment

al constructions can be categorised depending on the kind of commitment
they emphasise. Broadly speaking, we classify instances of modality as
onging to one of three modal domains, each of which highlights a different
type of function and provides a different sense of meaning.

Deontic modality

These expressions highlight a sense of obligation or necessity, for example:

> You *must* come back (modal auxiliary verb)

> It is *necessary* for you to come back (modal adjective)

Boulomaic modality

These expressions highlight aspects of desire, for example:

> I *hope* you will come back (modal lexical verb)

> *Hopefully,* you will come back (modal adverb)

Epistemic modality

These expressions highlight degrees of belief, certainty or perception,
for example:

> You *might* come back (modal auxiliary verb)

> I *think* you'll come back (modal lexical verb)

> You'll come back, *I guess* (modal tag)

> It's *clear* that you are coming back (modal adjective)

KEY TERMS

Deontic modality: expressions that highlight a sense of obligation or
necessity

Boulomaic modality: expressions that highlight aspects of desire

Epistemic modality: expressions that highlight degrees of belief,
certainty or perception

It's worth remembering that these are broad categories and some verbs can
behave in different ways depending on how they are used. For example, 'must'
can have both a deontic and an epistemic sense as demonstrated below.

- *you must leave now* (deontic sense showing necessity)

- *This must be the one we are looking for* (epistemic sense showing a degree
  of certainty)

The stylistician Paul Simpson provides a very useful model for categorising and exploring the effects of modality in texts. In this model, Simpson (1993) distinguishes between:

- modes of telling

- modes of seeing

- shades of modality.

Simpson argues that narratives may be told either in the first person (homodiegetic) or the third person (heterodiegetic); the viewpoint may be that of the narrator or be filtered through the consciousness of a character. And narratives may be classified on what he terms their dominant modal shading:

- **Positively shaded narrative**: the prominent use of deontic and boulomaic forms, and/or epistemic forms that show strong certainty together with evaluative adjectives and adverbs.

- **Negatively shaded narrative**: the prominent use of epistemic forms that display uncertainty and/or anxiety.

- **Neutrally shaded narrative**: a flat narrative with little or no modalised expressions.

Read Text 3H, an extract from Susan Hill's ghost story *The Woman in Black*. In this extract, the narrator is reflecting on the strange events he has witnessed at Eel Marsh House.

Text 3H

For a moment I actually began to conjecture that there was indeed someone – another human being – living here in this house, a person who hid themselves away in that mysterious nursery and came out at night to fetch food and drink and to take the air. Perhaps it was the woman in black? Had Mrs Drablow harboured some reclusive old sister or retainer, had she left behind a mad friend that no one had known about? My brain span all manner of wild, incoherent fantasies as I tried desperately to provide a rational explanation for the presence I had been so aware of. But then they ceased. There was no living occupant of Eel Marsh House other than myself and Samuel Daily's dog. Whatever was about, whoever I had seen, and heard rocking, and who had passed me by just now, whoever had opened the locked door was not 'real'. No. But what was 'real'? At that moment I began to doubt my own reality.

Extract from *The Woman in Black*, Susan Hill, Vintage (1998)

This extract is an example of a negatively shaded narrative. Its prominent features include the epistemic modal lexical verbs 'conjecture' and 'doubt', and the epistemic modal adverb 'perhaps', as well as evaluative forms such as the adjective 'mysterious', the pre-modified noun phrase 'wild, incoherent fantasies' and the series of questions that the narrator asks himself. The modal shading here offers a way of highlighting how Susan Hill portrays the uncertainty of her narrator and the representation of his mind at a time when he is unaware of what he has just experienced.

> **KEY TERM**
> **Modal shading:** the dominant type of modality in a text

3.4 Transitivity

One of the central tenets of stylistics is that all language choices are significant. For example, a sentence such as 'After lunch, Emily went to find her friend' involves a writer or speaker choosing to use the noun 'lunch' rather than a specific time, the proper noun 'Emily' rather than a less specific noun phrase such as 'the girl' or the pronoun 'she', the past tense verb 'went' instead of the present tense or the profiling of a different action such as 'walked' or 'rushed', and so on.

In all of these instances, the choice of one particular lexical item or phrase excludes many other possible ones. So, for example, this same event could have been represented by 'At 1.30 p.m., the young woman rushed to seek her out' (in this instance individual words have been replaced) or by 'She was found by her friend Emily at 1.30 p.m.' (in this instance some changes at word level have been made in addition to the sentence being reframed in the passive voice; see Chapter 2).

Individual choices that text producers make are significant in that they often contribute to patterns, which can help us to understand how texts operate and may give rise to particular interpretative effects. For example, Text 3I is an extract from an action thriller by Lee Child. In this extract, the main protagonist Reacher is represented largely through a series of actions: 'moved forward', sliding', came up', 'worked out', 'jammed'. There is only one verb process, 'feeling', that denotes some kind of mental operation. Of course, in this particular genre, we would expect actions to dominate since characters are largely defined by what they do. The representation of Reacher as a 'thinker' in this extract (and indeed across this novel) would be at odds with our expectations of the genre and the role that Reacher plays within it.

Text 31

Reacher moved forward, carefully sliding his feet flat on the floor, feeling his way with the toes of his boots. He came up against the first guy's head, and worked out where his gut must be, and jammed the shotgun muzzle down into it hard.

Extract from *Worth Dying For*, Lee Child, Bantam (2010)

A useful mode for examining patterns in the ways that characters are represented at the level of the clause draws on Michael Halliday's transitivity system (Halliday and Matthiessen 2004). Within any clause we can distinguish between processes (verb phrases), participants (noun phrases) and circumstances (usually prepositional and adverb phrases). For example:

The lecturer	handed out	the books	slowly.
participant	process	participant	circumstance

In Chapter 2, we identified four types of process: material, relational, mental and verbal. The remainder of this section outlines these processes in more detail, and introduces a further two processes that Halliday includes in his model: behavioural and existential processes. What follows is a much simplified version of what is quite a complex model. For each process, the participant roles have also been identified.

A material process shows physical actions and events with two participant roles: an actor (the 'doer' of the action); and the goal (the entity the action is directed at and is affected by the process).

John	kissed	Mary.
actor		goal

In contrast, a relational process is descriptive in that it assigns an attribute to an entity (roles of carrier and attribute) or identifies some aspect of it (roles of identified and identifier).

This bread	is	stale.
carrier	process	attribute

Jane	is	the leader.
identified	process	identifier

An existential process is similar to a relational process in its descriptive function but tends to be introduced by what is known as a dummy subject ('It' or 'There') and includes an existent role.

> There   was   a storm.
> dummy subject   process   existent

Whereas a material process denotes actions that occur in the physical world, a mental process refers to experiences of emotion, knowing and perception, all of which occur in the mind. A mental process has two participant roles: a senser (the person in whose mind the process occurs) and the phenomenon (a fact, object, idea, etc.).

> I   love   you.
> senser process phenomenon

> I   knew   the answer.
> senser process phenomenon

A behavioural process exists at some point between a material and a mental process, showing the outward physical signs of some internal process. A behavioural process has a behaver (the participant behaving).

> He laughed.
> behaver

In a similar way, a verbal process sits in between a material and a mental process but presents the outward behaviour of a form of speech.

> I screamed at John.
>
> sayer   receiver

KEY TERMS

Behavioural process: a process that shows the outward display of some initial internal process

Verbal process: a process that presents speech

ACTIVITY 3.3

Identifying processes and participants

Read Text 3J, the opening of *Tom Sawyer* by Mark Twain.

Identify all the processes and participants you can see. Is there a pattern in the kinds of processes used? How does this pattern help to build a sense of character?

Text 3J

"Tom!"

No answer.

"Tom!"

No answer.

"What's gone with that boy, I wonder? You TOM!"

No answer.

The old lady pulled her spectacles down and looked over them about the room; then she put them up and looked out under them. She seldom or never looked THROUGH them for so small a thing as a boy; they were her state pair, the pride of her heart, and were built for "style," not service— she could have seen through a pair of stove–lids just as well. She looked perplexed for a moment, and then said, not fiercely, but still loud enough for the furniture to hear:

"Well, I lay if I get hold of you I'll—"

She did not finish, for by this time she was bending down and punching under the bed with the broom, and so she needed breath to punctuate the punches with. She resurrected nothing but the cat.

"I never did see the beat of that boy!"

She went to the open door and stood in it and looked out among the tomato vines and "jimpson" weeds that constituted the garden. No Tom. So she lifted up her voice at an angle calculated for distance and shouted:

"Y–o–u–u *Tom*!"

There was a slight noise behind her and she turned just in time to seize a small boy by the slack of his roundabout and arrest his flight.

Extract from *Tom Sawyer*, Mark Twain (1876)

3.5 Deixis and viewpoint

Readers often talk of being immersed in the world of the novel, poem or play that they are reading. This results in an ability to empathise with characters and their situations and take on their particular points of view in relation to the fictional events that occur around them. In this section, you will explore the specific expressions that help to create particular perspectives within the text. This is a feature of language known as deixis. Deictic words are words that are context-bound in so far as their meaning depends on who is using them, where they are using them and when they are using them. For example, if you say the words 'I am here today' sitting in Birmingham on 1 February 2017, the deictic centre consists of a person (I), place (Birmingham) and time (1 February 2017). But, if you say those words in a different place and at a different time, then the words 'here' and 'today' will refer to a different place and time zone. If instead of you, someone else says these words, then the time and place to which they refer will differ again.

Deictic terms belong to one of a number of categories. The three main deictic categories are:

- **person deixis** (e.g. names and personal pronouns)

- **spatial deixis** (e.g. adverbs of place such as 'here', 'there', demonstratives showing location such as 'this' and 'that', and deictic verbs such as 'come' and 'go')

- **temporal deixis** (e.g. temporal adverbs such as 'today', 'yesterday' and 'tomorrow', prepositional phrases such as 'in two hours', 'in two weeks time').

KEY TERMS

Deixis: words that are context-bound and whose meaning depends on who is using them, and where and when they are being used

Deictic centre: the origin of an expression from which the expression points out and is understood

Deictic categories: types of deictic expressions (**person, spatial** and **temporal**)

In fact, returning to 'I am here today', we can see that there are various combinations in which all three deictic centres (person, spatial and temporal) could be configured. For example, it's possible to say the same words on 2 February, in which case only the temporal deictic centre shifts, or in a different location, in which case only the spatial deictic centre shifts, and so on.

Deictic expressions can also signal degrees of proximity. In the example above, 'today' is temporally close to the speaker, while 'tomorrow' is more distant. Since deictic terms point outwards from a deictic centre, the concept of closeness is a useful one in distinguishing between deictic terms across all three categories. For example, you can also distinguish between the proximal and distal deictic pairs 'here' and 'now', 'this' and 'that', and 'these and those'. Figure 3.2 summarises these and shows the relationship between these expressions.

Figure 3.2: Categories of deixis

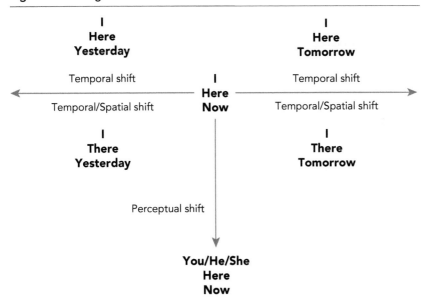

Deictic expressions play an important role in establishing and maintaining narrative viewpoint. In Text 3K, an extract from *City of Glass*, the first book in Paul Auster's *The New York Trilogy*, the protagonist Quinn is waiting at a train station. He is hoping to find a man called Stillman whom he has been employed to follow.

Text 3K

Quinn watched them all, anchored to his spot, as if his whole being had been exiled to his eyes. Each time an elderly man approached, he braced himself for it to be Stillman. They came and went too quickly for him to indulge in disappointment, but in each old face he seemed to find an augur of what the real Stillman would be like [...].

Extract from *City of Glass*, Paul Auster, Faber (1985)

Here, the reader needs to shift their own perspective (i.e. as a real-world living person) to that of the fictional character. In this extract, the point of view the reader is asked to adopt is clearly that of Quinn, even though the story is narrated in the third person. This perspective anchors Quinn as the perceptual deictic centre through the consistent use of the proper noun 'Quinn' and the pronoun 'he'. The deictic centre is also maintained through the use of the deictic verbs 'approached', 'came' and 'went', which are all processes of movement either towards the deictic centre ('approached' and 'came') or, as in the case of 'went', away from it. These deictic verbs help to position readers to adopt the same viewpoint as Quinn.

In this extract, the point of view and time frame remain constant. However, authors can manipulate these parameters by asking readers to shift between particular deictic fields, from one perceptual, temporal or spatial centre to another, as they read. This is known as a deictic shift (Segal 1995). One obvious way that a deictic shift occurs is via a change in point of view, or location, or the setting up of an alternative time frame. Inevitably, this happens in all texts at some point; indeed a few pages later in *City of Glass*, a new chapter beginning with 'The next morning' signals that the narrative events are now in a different time frame. Consequently, the reader must now re-imagine a new scene away from the time and location of the previous chapter and relate their reading from that point on in relation to this new temporal deictic centre.

KEY TERM

Deictic shift: a movement between particular deictic fields, from one perceptual, temporal and/or spatial centre to another

---

A phrase such as 'The next morning' acts as a deictic shift device. Similarly, newly mentioned proper nouns or pronouns, adverbs such as 'there' and 'then', and any shifts in verb tense would also initiate a deictic shift. On the other hand, the repetition of a name, a constant focus on a location or people and entities in it, and a consistent time frame would all act as anti-shift devices and maintain the deictic centre. For example, in Text 3K, 'Quinn' and 'he' act as prominent anti-shift devices that allow the reader to consistently adopt the character's viewpoint throughout the scene.

ACTIVITY 3.4

Exploring deictic shifts

Read Text 3L, 'La belle dame sans merci' by the nineteenth-century poet John Keats (note: there is a glossary at the end of the poem). In this poem, stanzas 1–3 are spoken by an unknown narrator and stanzas 4–12 are spoken by the knight-at-arms.

Identify any deictic shifts that you can find in the poem. What are they? How do they contribute to your understanding of the poem? What do you notice about the end of the poem in terms of where the deictic centre is? What effect do you think that has?

Text 3L

O what can ail thee, knight-at-arms,
    Alone and palely loitering?
The sedge has withered from the lake,
    And no birds sing.

O what can ail thee, knight-at-arms,
    So haggard and so woe-begone?
The squirrel's granary is full,
    And the harvest's done.

I see a lily on thy brow,
    With anguish moist and fever-dew,
And on thy cheeks a fading rose
    Fast withereth too.

I met a lady in the meads,
    Full beautiful—a faery's child,
Her hair was long, her foot was light,
    And her eyes were wild.

I made a garland for her head,
    And bracelets too, and fragrant zone;
She looked at me as she did love,
    And made sweet moan

I set her on my pacing steed,
    And nothing else saw all day long,
For sidelong would she bend, and sing
    A faery's song.

She found me roots of relish sweet,
    And honey wild, and manna-dew,
And sure in language strange she said—
    'I love thee true'.

She took me to her Elfin grot,
    And there she wept and sighed full sore,
And there I shut her wild wild eyes
    With kisses four.

And there she lullèd me asleep,
    And there I dreamed—Ah! woe betide!—
The latest dream I ever dreamt
    On the cold hill side.

I saw pale kings and princes too,
    Pale warriors, death-pale were they all;
They cried—'La Belle Dame sans Merci
    Thee hath in thrall!'

I saw their starved lips in the gloam,
    With horrid warning gapèd wide,
And I awoke and found me here,
    On the cold hill's side.

And this is why I sojourn here,
    Alone and palely loitering,
Though the sedge is withered from the lake,
    And no birds sing.

'La belle dame sans merci', John Keats (1819)

Glossary

ail	trouble
sedge	a grass-like plant
steed	horse
manna-dew	the heavenly food God gave the Israelites (manna), in liquid form (dew)
grot	cave
gloam	darkness
sojourn	stay

RESEARCH QUESTION
From page to screen

Choose a film or television adaptation of a book you have read and select a scene that allows you to explore the presentation of speech and/or thought. Compare how this has been presented in the written text and the screen version. How has the thought been translated into the visual medium and what stylistic effects do you think each version creates?

Repeat this activity to explore how film or television handles the other topics in this chapter: modality; transitivity; deictic shifts.

Wider reading

You can find out more about the topics in this chapter by reading the following books:

Speech and thought presentation

Leech, G. and Short, M. (2007) *Style In Fiction: A Linguistic Introduction to English Fictional Prose* (Second Edition). London: Longman.

Simpson, P. (2014) *Stylistics: A Resource Book for Students* (Second Edition). London: Routledge.

Modality

Palmer, F. (2001) *Mood and Modality* (Second Edition). Cambridge: Cambridge University Press.

Simpson, P. (1993) *Language, Ideology and Point of View*. London: Routledge.

Transitivity

Coffin, C., Donohue, J. and North, S. (2009) *Exploring English Grammar: From Formal to Functional*. London: Routledge.

Thompson, G. (2014) *Introducing Functional Grammar* (Third Edition). London: Routledge.

Deixis

Stockwell, P. (2002) *Cognitive Poetics: An Introduction*. London: Routledge.

Chapter 4
Stylistics and the mind

In this chapter you will:

- Explore some key topics in cognitive poetics

- Understand how to apply ideas from cognitive
  poetics to your stylistic analyses of texts

4.1 Introduction

This chapter introduces cognitive poetics, a branch of stylistics concerned with the application of knowledge about how the mind operates to understand the process of literary reading. Cognitive poetics was a term coined by Reuven Tsur, although currently the discipline of cognitive poetics bears a much stronger resemblance to the work of Peter Stockwell. Stockwell's key work *Cognitive Poetics: An Introduction,* first published in 2002, acts as the defining text for most stylisticians. Stockwell explains the term: 'cognition is to do with the mental processes involved in reading, and poetics concerns the craft of literature' (2002: 1).

> ## KEY TERM
>
> **Cognitive poetics:** a branch of stylistics concerned with the application of knowledge about how the mind operates to understand the process of literary reading

Cognitive poetics is concerned as much with mental representations that readers form when they read as with patterns in the text, and aims to link the two together. This chapter outlines and demonstrates the application of four cognitive poetic frameworks: figure-ground, schema theory, metaphor and Text World Theory.

4.2 Figure-ground

Figure-ground is closely related to the Russian Formalists' idea of foregrounding, which was introduced and discussed in Chapter 2. Foregrounding explains that when we read, certain things naturally draw our attention – or 'come to the fore' – whilst others tend to pass over relatively unnoticed. Figure-ground, like foregrounding, is centrally concerned with attention. It offers a cognitive account of the ideas the Russian Formalists came up with years before. In doing so, it enables us to explain and describe why some elements of a text tend to attract readers' attention more than others and, very usefully, why readers can read the same text and emerge with different interpretations depending on where they have focused their attention.

In the figure-ground model, whatever a reader is currently paying attention to forms the figure of their attention and everything else is left in the ground.

Look at the sentence in Text 4A.

Text 4A

John was sitting on a chair, a chair, a chair.

In this example, the deliberately repeated noun phrase 'a chair' shifts the figure of attention from the subject of the clause 'John'. At first 'John' was the figure but, through no longer being mentioned, quickly becomes the ground.

Whilst figure-ground is typically viewed as a binary system, it's actually a bit more nuanced than that. As Stockwell explains:

> it is a cline of prominence, ranging through degrees of foregrounding into vague, undifferentiated but rich background (Stockwell 2009: 31).

In other words, when we focus on 'chair' we do not immediately forget that we were focused on 'John' a moment before, and it would be possible for the figure-ground configuration to change again if, for example, 'John' was mentioned. As we move through our daily lives, therefore, and as we read, things constantly shift between the figure and the ground of our attention.

KEY TERMS

Figure: whatever forms the current focus of a person's attention

Ground: elements of any given scene which do not form the current focus of a reader's attention

Cline: a sliding scale between two extremes where examples can be somewhere in between rather than being one extreme or the other

---

4.2.1 Attention

Drawing on a huge body of research in Gestalt psychology, figure-ground explains that we are physically incapable of paying attention to everything in our visual range at once; that would be completely overwhelming and we would have no way to make sense of what we're seeing! Instead, we consciously and unconsciously select what we figure and what we leave in the ground.

Imagine looking at a huge crowd of people and then focusing on different individuals within the group. Here the crowd is initially our main figure and the rest of the scene – the floor on which they're standing, the sky, and any buildings or objects around – forms the ground. As you move to focus on an individual, however, the rest of the crowd joins part of the ground and the individual, in turn, becomes the figure. As you move to the next person, the first re-joins the crowd as part of the ground and the second person becomes the figure, and so on. You could switch your attention back to the first person and re-instantiate them as the figure. Another useful term here is attentional decay. This is what happens when you do not return to the first person and they quickly become lost in the crowd: they have 'decayed' from your field of attention.

KEY TERMS

Gestalt psychology: an area of research in visual psychology that explores how humans process what they see

Attentional decay: the process by which a figure moves out of the focus of attention and is replaced by a new figure

---

The same principle applies to any text we read – something is always the figure of our attention, the rest remains in the ground. Reading a text is like moving through the crowd and looking at each of the individuals: we move through a series of figures – some become more prominent as we repeatedly return to them, others we barely register at all; they stay for the most part in the ground.

So how do we decide what to figure and what to leave in the ground? Stockwell offers a list of features of good attentional attractors:

- **Newness** (new objects, characters, scenes, movements: the present moment of reading is more attractive than the previous moment)

- **Agency** (noun phrases in the active position are better attractors than in the passive position)

- **Topicality** (noun phrases in the subject position are more likely to be figures than those in the object position)

- **Empathetic recognisability** (human speaker $\longrightarrow$ human hearer $\longrightarrow$ animal $\longrightarrow$ object $\longrightarrow$ abstraction)

- **Definiteness** (definite ('the man') $\longrightarrow$ a specific indefinite ('a certain man') $\longrightarrow$ non-specific indefinite ('any man'))

- **Activeness** (verbs denoting action, violence, passion, wilfulness, motivation or strength)

- **Brightness** (lightness or vivid colours attract attention over dimness or drabness)

- **Fullness** (richness, density, intensity or nutrition)

- **Largeness** (large objects)

- **Height** (objects that are above others, are higher than the perceiver, or which dominate the scene)

- **Noisiness** (anything which makes sound or is noisy relative to other things in the scene)

- **Aesthetic distance from the norm** (beautiful or ugly referents, dangerous referents, alien objects denoted, unusual things)

(adapted from Stockwell 2009: 31)

KEY TERM

Attentional attractor: a characteristic of any text element that tends to encourage a reader to figure something as the focus of their attention

---

Read Text 4B, taken from the opening of Helene Dunbar's novel *These Gentle Wounds*, which illustrates how these attentional attractors also draw our focus in texts.

Text 4B

The last thing I saw before the car hit the water was an eagle pasted against the sky.

And what I remember is this: his tapered wings filled the width of the dirty window; the air held him up with the promise of magic; he looked free.

I used to dream about that bird.

But I don't have dreams anymore.

All I have are memories.

My arms are pinned. Water rushes up past my ears, and the kids cry in the backseat as they start to wake up. My mom's hands are wrapped around the steering wheel as she prays, saying words that make no sense but sound something like poetry.

Extracts from *These Gentle Wounds*, Helene Dunbar, Flux (2014)

This opening passage is told through the perspective of the novel's main character Gordie but, interestingly, he is almost never the figure of our attention. In this scene Gordie is recollecting being in a car with his mother and siblings when he was younger as it crashed into a river, but this is not immediately obvious, as young Gordie's attention moves from an eagle, to the water, to his younger siblings and finally to his mother, but never really focuses on the car or its position in the river.

First the eagle is encouraged as the figure of the reader's attention using the attractors of height, definiteness and empathetic recognisability. This figuring is intensified as the reader is given more and more information about the eagle – his wings, his 'promise of magic', the way he looks – and none about the car crash, encouraging them to leave this in the ground of their attention. The three shorter lines then gradually encourage the reader to shift the figure of their attention away from the bird and onto the 'memories'. Gordie's attention then sharply shifts – and the bold line breaking the paragraphs signals to the reader to do the same – from the outside to the inside of the car. However, Gordie still never focuses on the scene itself but only objects within it. After briefly figuring his own arms, the activeness ('rushes') and height ('up') of the water pulls the reader's attention, followed by the noisiness, first of 'the kids' in the back and then to the more definite figure of 'my mom'. Gordie's mother becomes the best and final attentional attractor in this scene because where 'the kids' remain a less definite group, she is represented as an individual. Like the kids she displays noisiness but her noisiness is more definite: the less distinct 'cries' cannot compete with the 'praying' in 'words that make no sense but sound something like poetry'.

Here you can see an excellent example of how an author has manipulated the reader's attention for effect. Dunbar disorients the reader by focusing on zoomed-in elements without giving a clear sense of the scene as a whole. In doing so, she mimics the protagonist's shock and disorientation by positioning the reader in the car with Gordie himself. Consider how different this scene might have been if an external narrator had focused attention on the car as it drove into the river, rather than with the character inside it.

ACTIVITY 4.1

Figure-ground

Read Text 4C, an extract from the opening of Alice Sebold's novel *The Lovely Bones*. The extract appears in the centre of its own page, just before Chapter 1. Analyse this extract in terms of figure-ground, commenting on how a reader's attention is drawn to specific entities in the text.

Text 4C

Inside the snow globe on my father's desk, there was a penguin wearing a red-and-white-striped scarf. When I was little my father would pull me into his lap and reach for the snow globe. He would turn it over, letting all the snow collect on the top, then quickly invert it. The two of us watched the snow fall gently around the penguin. The penguin was alone in there, I thought, and I worried for him. When I told my father this, he said, "Don't worry, Susie; he has a nice life. He's trapped in a perfect world."

Extract from *The Lovely Bones*, Alice Sebold, Picador (2002)

4.3 Schema theory

Schema theory makes claims about how people organise their background knowledge. Relevant associated chunks of our knowledge are formed into schemas, which we access in order to make sense of new situations on a daily basis. For instance, a person who has been to, or has been told about, restaurants is likely to know that meals are eaten there, what menus are, that a member of serving staff will assign tables and take orders, that money will be required to pay at the end. This is because the person has a 'restaurant schema'.

> **KEY TERM**
>
> **Schema:** a bundle of information about something that we hold in our mind

4.3.1 Elements of schema theory

Stockwell summarises the following as particularly useful to understanding schema theory:

- Schema accretion: where new facts are added to an existing schema, enlarging its scope and explanatory range.

- Tuning: the modifications of facts or relations within the schema.

  (Stockwell 2002: 79–80)

> **KEY TERMS**
>
> **Schema accretion:** the process by which new facts are added to an existing schema, enlarging its scope and explanatory range
>
> **Tuning:** the modifications of facts or relations within the schema

Schemas are dynamically constructed to suit specific new contexts. That is, schematic knowledge is not static but dynamic and, as new information accretes, it might cause a person to tune other stored information. Schemas can also be tuned to fit individual types of things, such as restaurants for example.

If a person has never been to Nando's, a popular restaurant chain specialising in chicken, they might walk in, sit at a table and wait for someone to come and take their food order. However, Nando's requires customers to go to the till to place food orders: the generic restaurant schema has not supplied all the necessary information needed for a successful visit. The new customer is unlikely to sit indefinitely waiting for a waiter or waitress: eventually they are likely to notice other customers going up to the counter, receiving their food shortly afterwards. In other words, this deviation from the generic restaurant schema is likely to be realised eventually. This new knowledge will be accreted to the Nando's schema and next time the person goes to Nando's they will know to order at the counter. There will be no need to re-enact the process and realise the differentiation from the generic schema again.

Schematic knowledge can be accreted from other people as well as from direct experience. For instance, a person who has never been to Nando's will know to order at the counter if they have read the previous paragraph. Schematic knowledge can also be easily called up without being physically present in the relevant context. Nor do people tend to get confused, for example, about the distinct features of different restaurant chains. This demonstrates that, in addition to a generic restaurant schema, individual restaurant schemas exist and are somehow coherently organised. It is possible to think about any restaurant chain and enjoy immediate access to a host of related information as well as rapidly switch between thinking about different restaurants without issue. This additionally demonstrates some sort of structured organisation. Humans can call up not just individual pieces of information but units of related information with ease, and without having to pore over other irrelevant bits of knowledge such as the day's news, thoughts about an old family cat or the shape of a watering can. This shows that background knowledge is not simply disorganised chaos.

Schema theory claims that headers are features which prompt us to activate certain schemas. Headers could be particular words or phrases that denote or connote objects, events, even actions. Many headers are highly ambiguous: they suggest multiple possible schemas we may need to activate to make sense of the scene. For instance, the phrase 'I ran' could suggest a sporting event, that the 'I' character is late or in a hurry, or even that there is some threat that the 'I' is running from. Other headers, typically more obscure lexical items, point to one schema in particular precisely because they do not tend to crop up in any other context: 'gavel' for instance nearly always suggests either a courtroom, some context to do with the law, or an auction.

KEY TERM

Header: a feature which prompts us to activate certain schemas

Often therefore it is not just the word or phrase that acts as the header, but the word or phrase alongside other words and phrases – other headers – or else the word or phrase *in context*.

4.3.2 Schemas and reading

Schemas were first discussed in relation to the cognition of literature by Frederic Bartlett (1932) in a catalogue of psychological experiments involving memory. In the key study, Bartlett asked participants to read a Native American folktale called 'The War of the Ghosts'. The story differed in many ways from a typical Western fairytale and, when Bartlett's participants were asked to recount the story a week after reading it, he found that these unusual features were often misremembered as their more typical counterparts. The story did not have a clear resolution as most Western folktales do but upon their retelling many participants reframed the story to give it just such a resolution. Unusual features with no real equivalent in traditional Westernised tales tended to be forgotten. This, Bartlett claimed, proved that the participants were drawing on some sort of pre-existing 'fairytale schema' when they read 'The War of the Ghosts' and that the passage of time had caused some of these unique tunings to decay from memory. When this happened the readers were replacing these features with information from their prototypical fairytale schema.

Schema theory offers a descriptive tool which enables an analysis to produce a convincing account of the ways in which readers subjectively understand and respond to texts whilst still being fundamentally text-driven. Read Text 4D.

Text 4D

Once upon a time, in a land far, far away.

Here, with no extra contextual detail about the story, most readers will activate a generic 'fairytale schema'. This may include a whole host of features they prototypically associate with fairytales, and which are based on their experience with this genre throughout their lives. As they read, they will likely have to 'tune' this schema to fit the specific fairytale they encounter, and may well 'accrete' features they have not encountered before, which will then be available to them for the next fairytale they encounter.

Now look at Figure 4.1.

This novel is based around the assassination of US President John F. Kennedy on 22 November 1963. The cover offers multiple potential headers, but the schematic knowledge each reader brings to viewing it will determine which schemas are activated. The title of the novel refers to the American date system, where the month is situated prior to the day. Here, schematic knowledge is vital as to whether or not the reader recognises the significance of the date, and indeed whether or not they recognise it as a date at all. They may even activate knowledge that situates the novel as American. Some readers will recognise the title as the date J.F.K. was assassinated, interpret it as a header, and activate their schema of knowledge for this event. Others will not, passing over it.

Figure 4.1: Cover of Stephen King's (2011) novel *11.22.63*

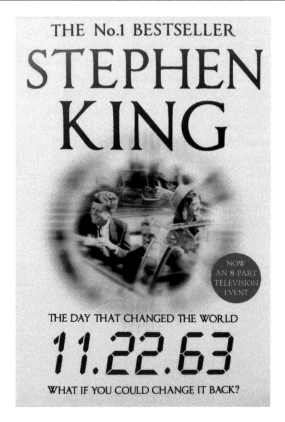

The cover demonstrates the multimodal nature of schema activation – that is, how images as well as text can activate schemas. This particular cover shows J.F.K. and his wife Jackie in an iconic shot; in the very motorcade in which they were travelling moments before he was assassinated. This may also serve as an effective header, pointing the reader to their store of knowledge regarding the Kennedy assassination. This may lead them to review the title and recognise it as another header pointing to this historical event. Equally, the tagline 'The day that changed the world. What if you could change it back?' may direct readers to review their schematic knowledge of 'days that changed the world' – and those who fail to identify the Kennedy assassination specifically may begin to activate their schemas for other significant historical events, perhaps involving a man and a woman, as denoted in the image.

Less obvious, is the single potential header 'What if you could change it back?'. This gesture towards the possibility of disrupting the timeline and changing the course of history may lead readers to activate their 'time travel' schema.

In conjunction with Stephen King's name, those who miss the references to J.F.K's assassination may, in activating their knowledge of King as predominantly a fiction writer, assume that the event being referred to is entirely fictional. Thus, whilst all interpretations are in some way grounded in the cover as a text, interpretations depend on the schematic knowledge each reader brings to viewing it, and thus which schemas are activated as a result.

Schema theory can be particularly useful to explain how readers go about orienting themselves and making sense of a text as it begins. Here, readers have not yet built up a sense of what the text is about, knowledge which will later inform and support their understanding of what the author is describing. This is especially true in the case of reading science fiction or fantasy texts, because these genres typically throw readers into a new world, or version of it, where they are initially unsure of the rules governing this new fictional space, and of what creatures may inhabit it. When this happens, we take cues from the text to activate our more general knowledge schemas, sometimes having to switch between them several times until we make sense of what we are 'seeing' in the text.

ACTIVITY 4.2

Schemas and interpretation

Read Text 4E, the opening paragraph to Daniel Keyes' novel *Flowers For Algernon*. The protagonist and narrator, Charlie Gordon, is a man of low IQ who is selected by a group of scientists as a candidate for an experimental drug designed to increase his intelligence. How might a reader rely on their schematic knowledge to make sense of the scene? How are the schemas they activate crucial to interpretation?

Text 4E

progris riport 1 martch 3

Dr Strauss says I shoud rite down what I think and remembir and evrey thing that happins to me from now on. I dont no why but he says its importint so they will see if they can use me. I hope they use me becaus Miss Kinnian says mabye they can make me smart. I want to be smart. My name is Charlie Gordon I werk in Donners bakery where Mr Donner gives me 11 dollers a week and bred or cake if I want. I am 32 yeres old and next munth is my birthday [sic]. I tolld dr Strauss and perfesser Nemur I cant rite good but he says it dont matter he says I shud rite just like I talk and like I rite compushishens in Miss Kinnians class at the beekmin collidge center for retarted adults where I go to lern 3 times a week on my time off. Dr. Strauss says to rite a lot evrything I think and evrything that happins to me but I cant think anymor because I have nothing to rite so I will close for today . . . yrs truly Charlie Gordon.

Extract from *Flowers for Algernon*, Daniel Keyes, Gollancz (1966)

4.4 Metaphor

4.4.1 Conceptualising through metaphor

Although this is a book on the language of literature, it is very important to remember that metaphor is not simply a literary phenomenon. In fact, much of the everyday language we use and many of the discourses and texts we encounter rely heavily on metaphor. For example, look at Text 4F, taken from a conversation between two friends discussing a relationship.

Text 4F

Speaker 1:	Take your time. Where's he going?
Speaker 2:	You know what I mean. Why do I think like that?
Speaker 1:	After you're engaged and all he's over here
Speaker 2:	No I have my whole life ahead of me so why am I…
Speaker 1:	You're rushing it

Taken from the Cambridge English Corpus

In this example, Speaker 2 speaks of her life as a kind of journey, understood in the sense of moving ahead spatially and temporally in the same way as we move physically. This way of representing an abstract concept (life) in concrete terms (a journey) is seen in expressions such as 'I'm getting on with my life', 'I'm moving forwards in life' as well as in the way distinct parts of life such as relationships and careers can be conceptualised. For example, expressions such as 'our relationship ended' and 'my career took off' similarly conceptualise the abstract through the concrete.

Although there is now a great deal of work on metaphor in stylistics, two early publications in the field, Lakoff and Johnson (1980) and Lakoff and Turner (1989), remain key texts on the cognitive approach to metaphor. This approach draws on cognitive linguistics more generally in understanding metaphor as the way that we organise and understand complex abstract concepts in terms of more physical ones. It views metaphors as not simply a question of language but as making visible the thought processes that both underpin language and affect our conceptualisations and representations of the world. The examples already looked at are instances of such a conceptual metaphor – LIFE IS A JOURNEY (conceptual metaphors are conventionally presented in small capitals in an X IS Y structure).

KEY TERM

Conceptual metaphor: a structure that presents one concept in terms of another

---

4.4.2 Source and target domains

As you have seen, a conceptual metaphor relies on explaining the abstract through the concrete. This can be explained more precisely by thinking about how one domain of knowledge is understood through another one. In conceptual metaphor, a target domain is given structure and meaning by a source domain.

In the conceptual metaphor LIFE IS A JOURNEY, the source domain 'journey' provides the structure for the target domain 'life' through the process of mapping, whereby elements of our journey schema are used to understand corresponding elements in the target domain. This provides a structure for conceptualising life, as Table 4.1 shows.

Table 4.1: LIFE IS A JOURNEY (adapted from Giovanelli 2014: 70)

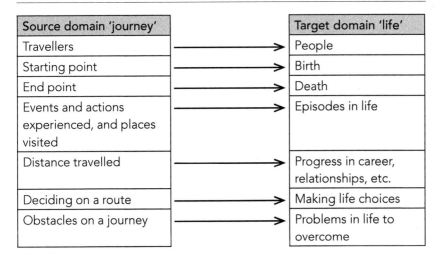

Source domain 'journey'	Target domain 'life'
Travellers	People
Starting point	Birth
End point	Death
Events and actions experienced, and places visited	Episodes in life
Distance travelled	Progress in career, relationships, etc.
Deciding on a route	Making life choices
Obstacles on a journey	Problems in life to overcome

KEY TERMS

Target domain: the concept that is understood through another domain of knowledge (source domain)

Source domain: a domain of knowledge used as a vehicle for understanding another concept (target domain)

Mapping: the process in which elements of the source domain are structured and understood through corresponding elements in the target domain

---

In the conceptual metaphor, the concept of life is understood as having a starting point (birth), an end point (death) and a series of episodes and experiences in between. Broader aspects of a journey, such as deciding on a destination, how far we travel and difficulties faced in reaching an end point are used to structure experiences in our lives. In fact, when we talk about our lives, we often use the same kind of language as when we talk about journeys. Furthermore, we can also see that we conceptualise our lives in this way: that is, the metaphor is a powerful tool that we use to make sense of 'living' in a day-to-day way.

As an example of this metaphor in literature, look at Text 4G, the first two stanzas from Robert Frost's poem 'The road not taken'. You can find the entire poem on the poetryfoundation.org website.

Text 4G

Two roads diverged in a yellow wood,

And sorry I could not travel both

And be one traveler, long I stood

And looked down one as far as I could

To where it bent in the undergrowth;

Then took the other, as just as fair,

And having perhaps the better claim,

Because it was grassy and wanted wear;

Though as for that the passing there

Had worn them really about the same

Extract from 'The road not taken', Robert Frost (1916)

The poem makes use of the LIFE IS A JOURNEY conceptual metaphor by presenting a scenario where the speaker has to make a choice between two paths. The roads present options on a journey in the same way as we have options in life. The need to make life choices is conceptualised in terms of weighing up the benefits of taking one particular pathway, 'And looked down one as far as I could', arguably here drawing on another common conceptual metaphor SEEING IS UNDERSTANDING. In this instance, the curve of the path in the undergrowth obscures complete vision in the same way as we cannot fully see into nor understand the future. We do, however, have to make life choices based on what knowledge is available to us. The poem as a whole presents life as a series of choices and draws on the concrete source domain of a journey with diverging pathways to remind readers that the decisions they take affect the rest of their lives.

Other common source and target domains that structure conceptual metaphors include the following (taken from Kövecses 2002: 16–25):

- **Common source domains**: the human body; health and illness; animals; plants; buildings and constructions; machines and tools; games and sport; business transactions; cooking and food; heat and cold; light and darkness; forces; movement and direction.

- **Common target domains**: emotion; desire; morality; thought; society; politics; the economy; human relationships; communication; time; life and death; religion; events and actions.

ACTIVITY 4.3
Source and target domains

Explore your understanding of metaphor by experimenting with Kövecses' list. Take any combination of a source and target domain, and write as many linguistic realisations of the conceptual metaphor as you can. You can be as creative as you want. For each one, explain how you feel the mapping operates, for example:

THOUGHT IS A PLANT

- The roots of my ideas

- My mind grew

- He planted a seed in my head

Of course, many of the examples of metaphor found in literary texts will be less conventional, where authors aim to foreground more innovative mappings between source and target domains. Read Text 4G, the first four lines from John Cooper Clarke's poem 'I wanna be yours'.

Text 4H

I wanna be your vacuum cleaner

breathing in your dust

I wanna be your Ford Cortina

I will never rust

Extract from 'I wanna be yours', John Cooper Clarke (2012)

In these lines, there are two overall metaphors:

- A PERSON IS A HOUSEHOLD APPLIANCE

- A PERSON IS A VEHICLE

In these lines, the source domains are evoked by the noun phrases 'vacuum cleaner' and 'Ford Cortina' (the Ford Cortina was a very popular car in the 1960s–1980s) as well as by the verb 'breathing' in line 2 and the verb 'rust' in line 4. The metaphorical mappings invite us to conceptualise the lovers and their relationship as being less than conventional. For example, vacuum cleaners are used to keep households clean, but the particular characteristic evoked, breathing in dust, suggests an element of possession on both sides (the speaker wishes to take in the lover but, as an appliance, would also be owned by him/her). Similarly cars are sat in and are used to travel, but they also protect. The claim to never rust invites an interpretation where the speaker is presenting him/herself as a reliable, caring and trustworthy partner, even if a little common (the choice of Ford Cortina rather than, say, a Ferrari)! The more we explore the mappings, the more we get a rich sense of the interpretative effects. A final and interesting point about the metaphors in this poem, which is linked to their novelty, is that both source and target domains are concrete entities. Unlike in the conceptual metaphors discussed so far, the target domain (a person) is not abstract.

4.4.3 Orientational metaphors

The examples of conceptual metaphor explored so far are all structural, in that they help the reader to conceptualise and understand one concept (the target domain) in terms of the structure of another (the source domain). George Lakoff and Mark Johnson (1980) also suggest that there is another kind of metaphor where a concept is understood spatially. For example, in the expressions 'I'm on a real high' or 'I'm feeling low', concepts (happiness or unhappiness) are understood as being vertically orientated (up versus down). Generally, orientational metaphors are motivated by the way our bodies exist and function in their spatial and social environments. For example, the orientational metaphors HAPPY IS UP; SAD IS DOWN have a physical basis: our bodies tend to be upright when happy but slump downwards when we are sad. An orientational metaphor is another example of the important connection between the social and physical world we inhabit and the ways in which we use language.

KEY TERM

Orientational metaphor: a metaphor where a concept is understood through spatial orientation

---

Other orientational metaphors include (from Lakoff and Johnson 1980: 15–16):

HEALTH AND LIFE ARE UP; SICKNESS AND DEATH ARE DOWN

He's in *top* shape

He came *down* with the flu

MORE IS UP; LESS IS DOWN

My salary went *up*

Turn the central heating *down*

GOOD IS UP; BAD IS DOWN

Things are looking *up*

The share value *fell*

ACTIVITY 4.4

Exploring use of metaphor

Read Text 4I, a poem by Langston Hughes. What do you notice about the metaphors that he draws on?

Text 4I

Well, son, I'll tell you:

Life for me ain't been no crystal stair.

It's had tacks in it,

And splinters,

And boards torn up, And places with no carpet on the floor —

Bare.

But all the time

I'se been a-climbin' on,

And reachin' landin's,

And turnin' corners,

And sometimes goin' in the dark

Where there ain't been no light.

So boy, don't you turn back.

Don't you set down on the steps

'Cause you finds it's kinder hard.

Don't you fall now —

For I'se still goin', honey,

I'se still climbin',

And life for me ain't been no crystal stair

'Mother to son', Langston Hughes, knopf (1994)

4.5 Text World Theory

4.5.1 Imagining worlds

Readers often talk of being 'transported' into the world of the novel, poem or play or being 'lost' in a book. The act of reading literature itself involves imagining alternative states of being in rich fictional spaces. Often, we can build up such a vivid and detailed account of fictional worlds that they become as memorable as the actual world in which we live. For example, we can identify and empathise with characters and their predicaments, understand their emotions and will them on to act and believe in a certain way. Locations and societies in fictional worlds can become so well known that they can be talked about amongst groups of readers as though they were actual places with people living in them.

Text World Theory (Werth 1999; Gavins 2007) is a dynamic grammatical framework that explains how we create rich, immersive fictional worlds when we read and offers a way of showing the importance of a reader's background knowledge, memories, experiences and emotions. It provides a way of exploring both individual language choices and broader patterns across longer stretches of text. And, because it is a discourse grammar, it emphasises the importance of context in explaining how speakers/listeners and readers/writers communicate and shape meanings.

4.5.2 Discourse-worlds

Text World Theory analyses three different conceptual levels. Imagine that you are out sitting in a park somewhere, talking to your best friend. In this instance, the two of you share a discourse-world, the context within which your conversation takes place. The discourse-world will include entities that you can see and hear in your immediate surroundings, as well as information that you have accepted as being relevant to the subject of your conversation and which you 'hold' in your mind as you talk. This might be related to the purpose of your discussion and include ideas and points from earlier on in your conversation or from when you last met. The context (and therefore the discourse-world) is dynamic in the sense that it evolves as new information becomes important.

In this example, you and your friend share a discourse-world in the same time and location. This is true for most spoken interaction, with a few exceptions such as telephone conversations and Skype calls. When we are reading literature, however, in the vast majority of cases we do not share the same time and location as the other participant (the author).

Now imagine you are sitting at home reading Gillian Flynn's novel *Gone Girl*. In this situation, you as a reader are separated in both time and space from the author. Flynn published the book in 2012 (and therefore probably wrote it much earlier) and is American. In these kinds of scenarios, we say that there is a split discourse-world.

KEY TERMS

Discourse-world: the context in which communication takes place

Split discourse-world: a discourse-world where participants are separated in time and/or space

---

4.5.3 Text-worlds

The next stage of analysis is the text-world. Text-worlds are rich mental representations that are built up as discourse proceeds. Read Text 4J. Imagine the conversation with your best friend in the park goes something like this:

Text 4J

You:	It was good to meet Emma yesterday at the shopping centre.
Your friend:	Those presents she had were very expensive.
You:	She gave them to her brother you know. He was very happy.

In this example, you and your friend as discourse-world participants co-construct a text-world. This text-world specifies time and place (yesterday and at the shopping centre), characters (you, Emma, her brother) and objects (presents). Within the text-world, these aspects are known as world-building elements, which function to anchor the text-world's parameters.

> ## KEY TERMS
>
> **Text-world:** a rich mental representation that is built up as participants communicate
>
> **World-building elements:** elements in a text-world that specify time, location, characters and objects

Now read Text 4K, the opening to 'The Pier Falls', a short story by Mark Haddon. It describes a tragedy that occurs when a pier collapses at an English seaside resort.

Text 4K

> 23 July 1970, the end of the afternoon. A cool breeze off the Channel, a mackerel sky overhead, and, far out, a column of sunlight falling onto a trawler…
>
> Extract from 'The Pier Falls', Mark Haddon, Jonathan Cape (2016)

In this example, you as the reader and Mark Haddon as the author share a split discourse-world. The text-world set up in the short story can be summarised as follows:

Time: 23 July 1970, at the end of the afternoon

Place: 'off the Channel' – beach/sea?

Characters/objects: trawler

As you can see, the text-world is defined very specifically in terms of time but there are fewer explicit world-building elements related to place. You might want to think about the effect of opening a story in this way! In fact, a reader has to use their knowledge of the phrase 'off the Channel' (i.e. the English Channel) to infer that the location is by the sea and possibly a beach, supported by the mention of the 'trawler' in the third line.

It's evident, however, that readers use their own background knowledge in the form of memories, experiences and schemas (see section 4.3) to help flesh out the text-world. So, a reader would use their own experience (either direct or indirect) of being by the sea in the summer to imagine the fictional world being evoked by Mark Haddon. Of course, this means that although many readers' representations of this opening will be similar, there will also be differences, sometimes very subtle and sometimes more pronounced. For example, if you had never been to the seaside or seen representations of it on television, it's possible that you would struggle to imagine a richly defined world as you read the opening to this short story.

ACTIVITY 4.5
Schemas

You can test the importance of schematic knowledge by looking at the words below. What images do they evoke for you? You could start by sketching out what you imagine when you read these words and then try to explain what associations they have. What memories and experiences might you draw on if you read these in a text?

- beach

- ice cream

- coffee-bar

Text World Theory accounts for the fact that a reader will only need to use particular kinds of knowledge through what is known as the principle of text-drivenness (Werth 1999: 103). This acts as a kind of safety valve to ensure that only background knowledge activated by the text is used in building text-worlds.

KEY TERM

Principle of text-drivenness: the fact that the text controls the knowledge a reader needs to draw on

Read Text 4L, the next sentence from Haddon's short story.

Text 4L

The upper storeys of the Regency buildings along the front sit above a gaudy rank of coffee houses and fish bars and knick-knack shops with striped awnings selling 99s and dried seahorses in cellophane envelopes.

Extract from 'The Pier Falls', Mark Haddon, Jonathan Cape (2016)

In this extract, the text effectively controls the schematic knowledge that a reader draws on. So, in this case, only knowledge relating to Regency buildings (built in early nineteenth-century Britain) and the various kinds of shops and their wares to be found along a seafront would be activated; any knowledge a reader might have about cricket, American presidents or the works of Shakespeare, for example, will clearly not be triggered by the text and will not be used.

Text-worlds, like the discourse-world, are dynamic in that they can be updated through the addition of further information. For example, in Text 4L, noun phrases such as 'Regency buildings', coffee houses' and 'fish bars' further enrich the text-world whilst the verb process 'sit above' shows the relationship between them. Verb processes generally act as function-advancing propositions in driving a narrative forwards and updating the text-world. Returning to the example from spoken discourse, we can see the following function-advancing propositions (underlined) in Text 4M.

Text 4M

You: It was good <u>to meet</u> Emma yesterday at the shopping centre.

Your friend: Those presents she <u>had were</u> very expensive.

You: She <u>gave</u> them to her brother you know. He <u>was</u> very happy.

KEY TERM

Function-advancing propositions: verb processes that drive forward the narrative

---

Function-advancing propositions generally either denote actions/events/ behaviours (material or behavioural processes), for example 'meet' and 'gave', or else portray states of being or having (relational processes), for example 'had', 'were'. The distinction between the two is an important one as it differentiates between propositions that foreground activity and propositions that foreground description.

ACTIVITY 4.6

Function-advancing propositions: the effect of patterns

Text 4N contains the first two paragraphs from 'The Pier Falls', including the sentences you have already looked at. Read through this entire extract and identify all of the function-advancing propositions. Now comment on any pattern that you can see across the paragraphs. What might the interpretative significance of this pattern be?

Text 4N

---

23 July 1970, the end of the afternoon. A cool breeze off the Channel, a mackerel sky overhead, and, far out, a column of sunlight falling onto a trawler as if God had picked it out for some kind of blessing. The upper

storeys of the Regency buildings along the front sit above a gaudy rank of coffee houses and fish bars and knick-knack shops with striped awnings selling 99s and dried seahorses in cellophane envelopes. The names of the hotels are writ large in neon and weatherproof paint. The Excelsior, the Camden, the Royal. The word Royal is missing an o.

Gulls wheel and cry. Two thousand people saunter along the prom, come carrying towels and Tizer to the beach, others pausing to put a shilling in the telescope or to lean against a balustrade whose pistachio-green paint has blistered and popped in a hundred years of salt air. A gull picks up a wafer from a dropped ice-cream and lifts into the wind.

Extract from 'The Pier Falls', Mark Haddon, Jonathan Cape (2016)

4.5.4 World-switches

Sometimes, the updating of a text-world involves more than simply adding further characters or objects, or developing a narrative through a series of function-advancing propositions. A world-switch (Gavins 2007: 74) occurs when the deictic parameters of the initial text-world are more dramatically altered so that a new remote text-world is set up.

An obvious and common world-switch occurs when there is a shift in time. A temporal world-switch is realised through expressions such as temporal adverbs such as 'tomorrow', 'later' or locative expressions, for example 'after an hour', which draw attention to a new set of deictic parameters, remote from the initial text-world. For example, read Text 40, the final paragraph from 'The Pier Falls'. In this extract, 'Ten years after' shifts the time frame of the narrative forwards and the new text-world is imagined as remote from the initial text-world.

KEY TERMS

World-switch: a shift that draws attention to a new text-world with different deictic parameters

Temporal world-switch: a world-switch due to a shift in narrative time

---

Text 40

Ten years after the disaster the pier is brought down in a series of controlled explosions and over many months the remnants are lifted laboriously by a floating crane and towed to a marine breakers in Southampton. No other human remains are found.

Extract from 'The Pier Falls', Mark Haddon, Jonathan Cape (2016)

Sometimes world-switches can be fleeting and the reader returns to the initial text-world very quickly. On other occasions, the world-switch can be maintained so that the initial text-world fades away and the switched-world becomes the new main text-world. For example, in 'The Pier Falls', the reader never goes back to the time frame at the beginning of the story where the pier collapses. The story ends in a very different time zone: a possible effect of this is that at the end of the story readers feel remote from the time in which the tragedy took place.

Other kinds of world-switches occur when attention is drawn away from the initial text-world to a remote world. These can include instances of the following:

- **Spatial shifts**: realised through prepositional phrases or nouns that shift attention to a new location with different deictic parameters

- **Direct speech**: realised through quoted speech with a reporting clause that shifts attention to a new perspective and deictic centre to the new speaker

- **Modality**: realised through modal verbs, adjectives, adverbs and clauses that draw attention to an attitude towards actions, events or characters

- **Negation**: realised through negating particles. Negation forces the reader to conceptualise a remote world containing the positive counterpart that is then understood as negated

- **Hypotheticality**: realised through if-clauses that set up a new remote text-world

PRACTICE QUESTION
World-switches

Text 4P is an extract from towards the middle of 'The Pier Falls'. The extract describes a young boy who has fallen into the water (the 'flooded forest' refers to the wreckage of the pier that has fallen into the sea). Read through the extract and identify the various world-switches you can find. What effect do these world-switches have on you as a reader?

Text 4P

The boy of thirteen will not come out from the flooded forest because he knows that his sister is in there somewhere. He cannot find her. After thirty minutes he is hypothermic and feels desperately cold. Then, quite suddenly, he doesn't feel cold at all. This doesn't seem strange. Nothing seems strange anymore. He wants to take his clothes off but hardly has the energy to stay afloat. Out there, only yards away, the world continues – sunshine, boats, a helicopter. But he feels safe in here. He is not thinking about his sister any more. He cannot remember having a sister.

Extract from 'The Pier Falls', Mark Haddon, Jonathan Cape (2016)

RESEARCH QUESTION
Reader responses

There are many ways that you can explore the topics in this chapter. You could collect texts of your own and analyse them using the cognitive stylistic tools and methods outlined. An alternative suggestion would be to generate some data on reader responses to texts. Find a text or extract that you think is interesting and you have analysed, and ask readers to talk about their responses to it. You can then explore aspects of the text in conjunction with extra-textual (i.e. response) data. For example:

- Do they feel their attention is manipulated at any point in the text? You could try to explain this in terms of figure/ground.

- What knowledge do they feel they are drawing on or being asked to draw on? You could look at these responses in terms of schema theory.

- How do they react to conventional or unconventional metaphors and their effects? You could explain these in terms of conceptual metaphor.

- Are there distinctive patterns in world-building and/or world-switches that they find significant? You could explore these in terms of Text World Theory.

Wider reading

You can find out more about the topics in this chapter by reading the following:

Cognitive poetics

Gavins, J. and Steen, G. (2003) *Cognitive Poetics in Practice*. London: Routledge.

Stockwell, P. (2002) *Cognitive Poetics: An Introduction*. London: Routledge.

Figure and ground

Ungerer, F. and Schmid, H. (2006) *An Introduction to Cognitive Linguistics* (Second Edition). Abingdon: Routledge.

Schema theory

Mason, J. (2014) 'Narrative'. In P. Stockwell and S. Whiteley (eds) *The Cambridge Handbook of Stylistics*. Cambridge: Cambridge University Press, pp. 179–95.

Stockwell, P. (2003) 'Schema poetics and speculative cosmology', *Language and Literature* 12 (3): 252–71.

Metaphor

Kövecses Z. (2002) *Metaphor: A Practical Introduction*. New York, NY: Oxford University Press.

Lakoff, G. and Johnson, M. (1980) *Metaphors We Live By*. Chicago, IL: University of Chicago Press.

Semino, E. (2008) *Metaphor in Discourse*. Cambridge: Cambridge University Press.

Text World Theory

Gavins, J. (2007) *Text World Theory: An Introduction*. Edinburgh: Edinburgh University Press.

Giovanelli, M. (2013) *Text World Theory and Keats' Poetry: The Cognitive Poetics of Desire, Dreams and Nightmares*. London: Bloomsbury.

Werth, P. (1999) *Text Worlds: Representing Conceptual Space in Discourse*. London: Longman.

Chapter 5
Exploring stylistics

In this chapter you will:

- Explore three cutting-edge applications of stylistics: supporting creative writing, considering how real readers respond to texts and using computer software to aid analysis

- Understand how to apply your knowledge of stylistics to support your creative writing

- Explore how computers can be used to support literary analysis through 'corpus stylistics'

- Be introduced to the key areas you need to consider in order to study real reader responses to texts

5.1 Introduction

This final chapter explores three exciting areas within stylistics which have grown and developed in recent years: topics at the cutting edge of the discipline. It draws together the things you have been looking at throughout this book and introduces three ways in which you could apply what you have learnt. Each respective section outlines the key research and how you could apply your knowledge to the areas of creative writing, studying readers' responses to a text you want to analyse, and using computers to help you identify patterns across whole literary texts and beyond.

5.2 Creative writing and stylistics

So far this book has focused on how you can use your stylistic toolkit to help you analyse the work of others. The value stylistics offers to creative writing is slightly different to what it offers to literary analysis, though the practice of reflecting on the effects of linguistic choices remains the same. Where the key value of stylistics to the analyst of texts is the ability to closely and systematically reflect on how an author's choices have created a particular effect, in creative writing the author and analyst are one and the same. In other words, stylistics offers creative writers the opportunity to examine, analyse and play around with their own writing style, to understand how they are creating effects and how making different linguistic choices may affect the writing they produce. Two key researchers working at the intersection of creative writing and stylistics are Rob Pope and Jeremy Scott, and you can find details of their work in the wider reading list at the end of this chapter.

One way Rob Pope, in his seminal text *Textual Intervention*, suggests that as an author you can best understand the stylistic effects of your language choices is through rewriting. He explains that writers and analysts should approach any text by asking themselves 'What if the text were different?', then that they actively intervene to make it different, and then stand back and reflect on the effects the changes have made (Pope 1995: 4). These are called rewriting exercises.

KEY TERM

Rewriting exercises: the practice of making deliberate changes to a text, either your own or one by another author, and then reflecting on how those changes have altered the text. Also known as 'textual intervention', a term coined by Rob Pope.

You can perform rewriting exercises at the micro- or macro-level of a text. At the micro-level you could, for instance, alter some of the lexical choices and then reflect on how the different words alter the text. It can be useful to select a particular class of words – the nouns, verbs or adjectives, for example – and to change them in a consistent way. This could include substituting all the words with synonyms or antonyms.

You can even produce multiple versions of the original text making different types of changes and compare the effects of the different alterations. Consider, for example, this opening verse of Byron's poem 'Darkness', which he wrote after a volcanic explosion, imagining the last days of the Earth.

Text 5A

I had a **dream**, which was not all a **dream**.

The **bright** sun was **extinguish'd**, and the stars

Did wander darkling in the **eternal** space,

Rayless, and **pathless**, and the **icy** earth

Swung blind and blackening in the moonless air;

Morn came and went—and came, and brought no day,

And men forgot their **passions** in the **dread**

Of this their **desolation**;

Extract from 'Darkness', Lord George Gordon Byron (1816)

ACTIVITY 5.1
Creative rewriting: lexical choices
Study the two rewritings of Text 5A. Text 5B substitutes synonyms, Text 5C antonyms.

Now replace the words in bold in Text 5A yourself. A thesaurus can be really helpful for these exercises.

Text 5B

I had a **fantasy**, which was not all a **fantasy**.

The **shining** sun was **terminated**, and the stars

Did wander darkling in the **unending** space,

Dark, and **without direction**, and the **frosty** earth

Swung blind and blackening in the moonless air;

Morn came and went—and came, and brought no day,

And men forgot their **feelings** in the **terror**

Of this their **ruin**;

Text 5C

I had a **nightmare**, which was not all a **nightmare**.

The **dingy** sun was **awoken** and the stars

Did wander darkling in the **limited** space,

Bright, and **purposeful**, and the **sunny** earth

Swung blind and blackening in the moonless air;

Morn came and went—and came, and brought no day,

And men forgot their **apathy** in the **excitement**

Of this their **recreation**;

All of these rewriting exercises use deliberate changes to create a variable where the rest of the text remains constant. This helps you consider what effect those particular features were contributing to the original text by comparing it with the rewritten examples.

At the macro-level of a text, you could add in, delete, or alter entire plot points or characters. You could add traits or a history to a character and reflect on how this affects the story. In fact, there's a popular practice that occurs predominantly online called fanfiction where readers use a text they have read and enjoyed as inspiration for their own creative writing. This can include extending a story, borrowing characters or settings and writing new stories involving them, or altering elements of the original story and rewriting scenes to incorporate these changes. Fanfiction can commonly include alterations such as changing the gender of a character or adding events that happen to characters that are not covered in the original story.

KEY TERM

Fanfiction: writing inspired by another author's work which borrows elements of the original text

Rewriting and altering texts, especially at the micro-level, offers opportunities to isolate particular stylistic features – the ones you have changed – as another way to examine what effects the original choices created and how they contributed to the style of the text as a whole.

ACTIVITY 5.2
Creative rewriting: plot alterations

Select a text you enjoy and choose a character. Write a 'flashback' scene involving that character that occurred prior to the main plot. Make sure something dramatic or shocking happens in the scene. Try to make the character's behaviour in your scene consistent with the way you feel they are presented in the original text.

Now imagine that your scene was included as part of the original text. How would the addition of this scene change the text and the way you understand the character?

Now select a scene in the original text where something significant happens to your chosen character and imagine how the text and your understanding of the character would be altered if that scene was removed.

5.3 Reader response studies and stylistics

A growing number of stylisticians have become interested in how real readers respond to texts. That is, typically when we engage in literary analysis we draw on a few sources when constructing a response or interpretation:

- Our own analysis and response to the text

- Analysis and responses to the text put forward by an 'expert', such as a literary critic.

The first dimension of literary analysis is unavoidable, regardless of the approach we take. However, stylisticians have begun to recognise that the way they respond to a particular text or extract might not be representative of how people more generally might respond, especially since literary analysts by their very nature are highly trained readers. This has led to the conclusion by many researchers that investigating reader responses needs to include looking at responses other than their own or those of other experts. This debate has led to the widespread use of terms like real readers.

In this section you are going to explore the basics of how people interested in real reader responses decide what kind of responses they want to examine and how they go about accessing or generating them. This section is a good starting point if you're thinking about undertaking a reader response study yourself as it will outline the things you would need to think about and do, and the kinds of options available to you, but there isn't room here to go into detail about designing your own study.

There are three important questions any stylistician needs to ask themselves when undertaking a study involving the responses of real readers:

- What is my research question?

- What kind of data would enable me to answer that question?

- How can I practically and ethically obtain those data?

You're now going to briefly explore how to go about answering these three questions, then you'll have the opportunity to consider some examples of how stylisticians have studied real reader responses.

KEY TERMS

Reader responses: any record of a reader or readers' thoughts about a text; these could take the form of reviews, comments on an online forum or in a reading group, answers to a questionnaire or even responses in a focus group or interview

Real readers: members of the public; this term is usually used to refer to readers outside academia such as researchers, academic experts or literary critics

Research question: a short and clear question which accurately summarises what a study intends to explore: the question to be answered

---

5.3.1 Deciding on a research question

A research question is crucial to any study because it provides a clear focus to a project and enables the researcher to answer the second and third questions posed above. A good research question will be quite short and specific, and will be targeted on one single issue. Bad research questions are too broad and unfocused for any one study to answer, or would need time and resources which far exceed what the researcher has available. They might also include terms that are ambiguous or hard to define. Examples of bad research questions would include:

- How do women feel about the novels of Charles Dickens?

- What do readers think of Chinua Achebe's novel *Things Fall Apart*?

The first question is far too broad both in terms of the group of readers it seeks to study ('women') and the texts it aims to research the responses to ('the novels of Charles Dickens'). The term 'feel' is also highly ambiguous: it's not clear what the research project would actually investigate. The second question is a little more focused because it specifies one text in particular but it is still too broad: no one study, unless it is very large in scale, could offer a definitive and generalised account of what all readers think of any text. Equally the term 'think of' is quite vague. Research questions like this are problematic because they can set researchers up to fail or they can be misleading about what the project will show.

Better formulations of these questions will offer clear and accurate definitions of the group of readers to be studied and what aspect of their responses is going to be investigated. For example, the above questions could be:

- How do an all-female reading group discuss their emotional responses to Charles Dickens' novel *Bleak House*?

- What reasons do negative online reviewers offer to explain their dislike of Chinua Achebe's *Things Fall Apart*?

There will always be more than one way in which any research question could be investigated. Often researchers will start with a more general research question and revise it until they have focused on something they can realistically investigate. For example, the vague question 'How do women feel about the novels of Charles Dickens?' cannot be explored in full by any one study, but it could be transformed into lots of different smaller studies, depending on what the researcher is interested in.

Three popular techniques stylisticians use to gather reader responses in order to answer a specific research question include:

- interviewing readers

- recording reading groups

- collecting online reviews.

Each of these approaches will require the researcher to refine and reword their research question, and each has a different set of implications for the kind of reader responses that the researcher is going to be able to collect, as well as different ethical implications. You will learn more about ethics in the next section.

> **KEY TERM**
>
> **Ethical implications:** the possible impact a research project could have on any person involved with it, which needs to be carefully considered when designing a study. In particular, any conceivable harm that could be caused to either participants or the researcher themselves must be explored, and addressed, as potential implications of the research

5.3.2 Interviewing readers

Interviewing readers to ask them about their responses to a text you are interested in studying is a great approach if you want to find out specific things such as their responses to a particular passage or how much they knew about the author before they read the text and the impact this had on their reading. These kinds of topics are less suited to techniques such as recording a reading group because you have no guarantee that the group will discuss the thing you want to find out about, and you could end up wasting a lot of time and energy.

However, if you interview readers it is important to remember that you are actively prompting the responses you are going to analyse: your participants might never have considered how they felt about that passage or how their knowledge of the author affected their response to the text if you hadn't asked them. This means that you cannot make claims that the responses are natural: they cannot be said to represent how readers respond to your text when they read it on their own. You also have to bear in mind that readers will be conscious that they are part of a study and therefore might choose not to tell you about aspects of their response to a text, for instance if they think it will make them look silly, or they feel embarrassed, or they do not want to share something personal.

5.3.3 Recording reading groups

Recording a reading group, especially if the group already existed, is an excellent way of investigating how readers discuss a text with one another in a more natural and authentic setting than an interview. This is because you are capturing responses that would have taken place even if you were not researching them. As with interviews, you need to bear in mind that the fact the group know they are being recorded is likely to affect what they do or do not say. This is called the observer's paradox, where as soon as a researcher tries to investigate something, it risks changing the thing because participants are aware they are being researched. This is an issue that needs to be considered for nearly all reader response studies because covert recording – recording people without asking them and gaining their consent – is unethical.

KEY TERMS

Observer's paradox: a problem whereby a person or group is aware that you are researching what they do or say, and may consciously or unconsciously change their behaviour as a result of being aware that they are being observed

Covert recording: the unethical practice of recording people without their knowledge and consent

Consent: a person's informed agreement to be researched; in order to give their consent a person needs to know what the research is for and how their responses are going to be used

5.3.4 Collecting online reviews

The best way currently available to researchers to try and get access to responses from readers that have not been affected by the observer's paradox is to collect online reviews from sites such as *Amazon* or *Goodreads*. These responses already existed before the research project and so are unaffected by the observer's paradox. The responses are available to the public – the readers knew other people would read them – so it is still important to consider that the responses have been created for a particular purpose. However, this is generally considered to be the best way to get the most naturalised responses to a text.

There is a lot of disagreement about whether collecting such responses is ethical or not. Some people say that the readers were aware that their responses could be read by anyone and that by posting them online they are already consenting for them to be used. Others say that these readers posted their responses for a particular purpose, typically to offer others advice about whether to read a book or not, and as such they are not consenting for their words to be used in a research project. Let's explore ethical considerations in a bit more detail.

5.3.5 Ethical considerations

There are important ethical considerations involved with taking any one of the three approaches described above, and if you want to try any of them for yourself you will need to check with your school or university about which procedures and guidelines you need to follow. Any project which involves other people needs to have been carefully considered for any ethical implications. Is there any risk that the project could cause anyone harm or violate their rights?

You should always check with a teacher or lecturer about whether or not you need to have your project ethically approved. If it involves human participants you almost certainly will, although some institutions will allow you to collect online responses without formal ethical approval. Even if you are only planning to collect responses solely online *you still need to check* with someone in authority that it is within your institution's rules to proceed without ethical approval. This approval involves a designated person or committee reviewing your research plans and formally agreeing that what you plan to do is okay. All universities have their own ethical procedures and will usually have a committee that deals with all research proposals. If you want to undertake a reader response study at school, the best thing to do is ask your teacher what you need to do about ethical approval.

No matter where you are or what your research plans are, you will always need to consider whether you need the people who are taking part in your study to complete a consent form. Consent forms need to let your participants know that they do not have to take part if they don't want to, that they are free to withdraw from your study at any time, and that there will not be any negative consequences if they decide not to carry on. This is vitally important because if a person worries that something bad might happen if they choose not to be involved or to withdraw from your study, it could mean that they continue when they don't really want to take part: people can't freely give their consent when they feel pressured. So if, for example, you asked a friend to take part in your study, they would need to know that they could decide not to be involved or that they could change their mind and that it wouldn't affect your friendship. If a teacher was undertaking a research project involving their students, those students would need to be confident that they could choose not to be involved and it wouldn't affect their grades or the way they were treated by the teacher.

KEY TERMS

Ethical approval: formal permission to carry out a research project, usually granted by a designated person or committee at your school or university

Consent form: a clear and concise document that you will need any readers involved in your project to sign before you begin collecting any of their responses; consent forms should only be signed when a person is in possession of enough information to be accurately informed about what they are giving their consent to

A consent form will normally need to be accompanied by a participant information sheet, a short summary of the research project that lets prospective participants know what they are agreeing to be involved in. This is crucial because people cannot give informed consent without knowing what they are agreeing to. Participant information sheets need to include honest and accurate information about whether or not the identities of the people involved will be anonymous and what exactly is going to happen to any data you collect, including how long you plan to keep it and where. It is good practice to take steps to make sure everything you collect is kept secure and confidential. If this is not going to be possible it is vital to tell your participants this and explain why.

KEY TERM

Participant information sheet: a clear and concise document that accompanies a consent form giving a person enough information about your project for them to make a decision about whether or not they want to take part; participant information sheets should not exceed two A4 pages

5.4 Corpus stylistics

The final section of this chapter will explore corpus stylistics, which is an emerging branch of corpus linguistics. Corpus linguistics involves using computer software to analyse and identify patterns in large data sets, or corpora, and is 'one of the fastest growing methodologies in contemporary linguistics' (Gries 2009: 1225). The use of corpus analysis is a relatively recent innovation but it is a powerful tool, offering a systematic and rigorous way of identifying patterns in large data sets. That said, the software is of little value if used in isolation: it can reveal the 'what' but not the 'why'. Corpus methods therefore offer a mainly supporting tool – used but not relied upon.

KEY TERMS

Corpus linguistics: a branch of linguistics that involves the use of computer software to identify patterns across a large amount of text

Corpora: the plural of 'corpus'. A corpus is a collection of words to be examined by the corpus software. It could be a single text or a selection of texts. It will normally contain more text than it is realistically possible for a person to examine and identify patterns without the aid of the software

Corpus stylistics uses corpus linguistics to analyse stylistic features. The key advantage of this is that patterns can quickly and easily be identified across whole texts in a way that would be very difficult to achieve by going through a text manually. Thus, corpus stylistics offers the opportunity to uncover characteristics of an author's style or to look at the representation of a character or theme across a whole text. This wasn't really possible before this kind of software became available.

So how does it work? Typically, corpus stylistics involves putting an electronic copy of a literary text into a corpus program and using the software to either help identify patterns, such as frequent words or phrases, or to quickly support or reject patterns that seem to exist when the text is read 'manually'. Some links to free or online corpus programs are given in the research task and in the wider reading list at the end of this chapter. In Table 5.1, for example, are the most frequent three-word phrases (sometimes called clusters) in George Orwell's *Animal Farm*, and the number of times they each appear.

Table 5.1: The most frequent three-word phrases in George Orwell's *Animal Farm*

Rank	Frequency	Cluster
1	31	the animals were
2	24	of the farm
3	24	on the farm
4	22	all the animals
5	21	beasts of England
6	20	of the animals
7	20	there was a
8	19	the other animals
9	16	that they had
10	16	the animals had
11	15	of the windmill
12	14	the farm buildings
13	13	battle of the
14	13	four legs good
15	13	good two legs
16	13	it was a
17	13	legs good two
18	13	that it was
19	13	the battle of
20	12	and the animals

Corpus techniques have become another tool in the stylistic toolkit. Where stylistics was previously bound to small sections of texts by its own requirements for close, reported analysis, corpus software now enables the swift identification of patterns in large data sets such as high frequency words and phrases. Corpus stylistics tends to be used *alongside* more traditional close analysis. For example, we could consider the following passage from *Animal Farm*:

Text 5D

Napoleon stood sternly surveying his audience; then he uttered a high pitched whimper. Immediately the dogs bounded forward, seized four of the pigs by the ear and dragged them, squealing with pain and terror, to Napoleon's feet. The pigs' ears were bleeding, the dogs had tasted blood, and for a few moments they appeared to go quite mad. To the amazement of everybody three of them flung themselves upon Boxer. Boxer saw them coming and put out his great hoof, caught a dog in mid-air and pinned him to the ground. The dog shrieked for mercy and the other two fled with their tails between their legs. Boxer looked at Napoleon to know whether he should crush the dog to death or let it go. Napoleon appeared to change countenance, and sharply ordered Boxer to let the dog go, whereat Boxer lifted his hoof, and the dog slunk away, bruised and howling.

Presently the tumult died down. The four pigs waited, trembling, with guilt written on every line of their countenances. Napoleon now called upon them to confess their crimes.

Extract from *Animal Farm*, George Orwell (1945)

When considering the representation of the character Napoleon, traditional close stylistic analysis already provides a lot of insight. You might observe, for example, that in this extract he seems to have a lot of authority and power over the other animals, first because he is typically the active subject in sentences and second because, when other characters such as the dogs and Boxer are in the subject position, they are acting on his orders or on his behalf. Corpus stylistics, however, enables you to take this one step further and look to see if this is a pattern that occurs in the rest of the novel. You could do this by searching the word 'Napoleon' in the text. This would show you a concordance diagram, where the corpus software will alphabetically line up the words to the left and right of the word you searched. Figure 5.1 shows the start of the concordance diagram for the word 'Napoleon' in *Animal Farm*.

5

Figure 5.1: Concordance diagram for 'Napoleon' in *Animal Farm*

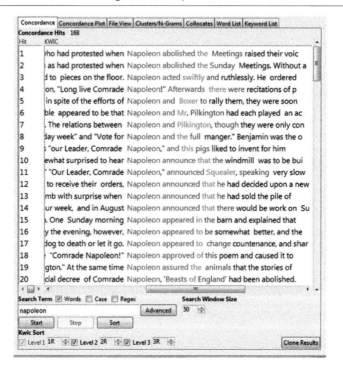

Here the corpus analysis reveals that Napoleon is indeed positioned as an active
subject, performing verbs that demonstrate his power over the other animals –
abolishing, acting, announcing and approving – not just in an isolated passage
but throughout the text.

Using this software you can also organise your concordance diagram
chronologically to look at all the instances of Napoleon's name in the text in
the order they appear. This could help you identify how early in the novella the
character begins to exert his power over the other animals (which is long before
he takes over the farm).

Corpus stylistics can be used the other way around, where the software can help you to identify patterns you would not otherwise have noticed in the text, enabling you to then look closely at the concordances to see if a pattern creates any stylistic effect.

The really important thing to remember, however, is that corpus software cannot do the stylistic analysis for you. It can help you see what patterns are present but it is still up to you to interpret them, and you might decide that a pattern you discover has no significance or stylistic impact at all. A good example of this is the idea that a corpus search of the words that appear immediately before Napoleon's name in *Animal Farm*, lined up alphabetically, will reveal that whenever Napoleon is mentioned with another character, Snowball, Orwell always places their names in the same order. In fact, 'Snowball and Napoleon' appears nine times in the text, and 'Napoleon and Snowball' never appears at all, as shown in Figure 5.2.

Figure 5.2: Concordance diagram for 'Snowball' and 'Napoleon' in *Animal Farm*

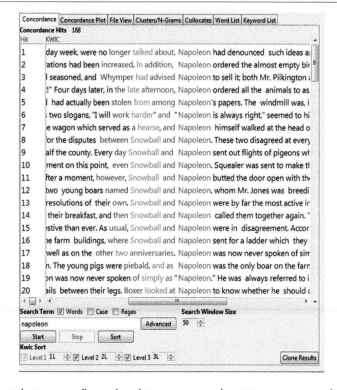

Corpus stylistics can tell you that this *is* a pattern, but it is up to you to decide if it has any significance.

RESEARCH QUESTION
A corpus search

Go to the CLiC website at clic.bham.ac.uk. This site has lots of books to choose from already loaded and ready for you to search. There is a wide variety of nineteenth-century British texts to choose from, including the complete works of Charles Dickens, Mary Shelley's *Frankenstein*, Bram Stoker's *Dracula*, Emily Brontë's *Wuthering Heights* or her sister Charlotte's *Jane Eyre*, and Jane Austen's *Pride and Prejudice*.

Click on 'Change Books' and choose a novel you'd like to research, preferably one you've read or know a little about. Now choose a character from that text. Before you search their name in the corpus, write down your impressions of the character based on your reading. What are they like and how would you describe them? Now search their name in the text and examine the concordances to the left and right, organised alphabetically.

Do these searches help you understand your impressions of the character? Can you spot any patterns? Look in particular for the adjectives used to describe them and the actions they perform in the verb phrases associated with them.

Wider reading

You can find out more about the topics in this chapter by reading the following:

Creative writing
Pope, R. (1995) *Textual Intervention: Critical and Creative Strategies*. London: Taylor and Francis.

Scott, J. (2013) *Creative Writing and Stylistics: Creative and Critical Approaches*. Basingstoke: Palgrave Macmillan.

Corpus stylistics
Anthony, L. (2014). AntConc (Version 3.4.3) <Computer Software>. Tokyo, Japan: Waseda University. Available from www.laurenceanthony.net/software.html

Brookes, G. and Harvey, K. (2016) 'Corpus linguistics'. In M. Giovanelli and D. Clayton (eds) *Knowing About Language: Linguistics and the Secondary English Classroom*. London: Routledge, pp. 125–36.

Gries, S. (2009) 'What is corpus linguistics?', *Language and Linguistics Compass*, 3: 1225–41.

Mahlberg, M. and Stockwell, P. (2016) 'Point and CLiC: teaching literature with corpus stylistic tools'. In M. Burke et al. (eds) *Scientific Approaches to Literature in Learning Environments*. Amsterdam: John Benjamins, pp. 251–67. Software available to use here: http://clic.bham.ac.uk/

Stockwell, P. and Mahlberg, M. (2015) 'Mind-modelling with corpus stylistics in David Copperfield', *Language and Literature*, 24: 129–147.

Ideas and answers

Chapter 1

Activity 1.1

Some of the distinctions between the two versions of the haiku which you might have commented on include:

- Both versions maintain the same number of syllables on each line, therefore both conform to the 5–7–5 structure of haiku.

- The characters 'tiger' and 'snake' remain the same in both. You might, however, have noted the change from indefinite articles to definite articles: 'a tiger' becomes 'the tiger' and 'a snake' becomes 'the snake'. You may have suggested that this makes the sense of character more definite in the second version, moving from actions any tiger or snake 'can' and 'will' perform in the first version to discussing the actions of a specific tiger and snake in the second. You might also have noticed that this change creates the impression that the reader has prior knowledge about which tiger and snake are being referred to, as the use of 'the' in noun phrases often indicates this.

- You may have considered the associations readers might make with these creatures and noted that they come from the same semantic field: animals.

- The changes to the main verb in line 1 from 'can' to 'may' and the modal auxiliary 'will' to 'might' in line 2 makes the second version much less definite. In Chapter 3 you will learn that this is a change to the epistemic modality in the poem. You might note that in the original version the snake's actions are presented as more likely to occur than the tiger's but that in the second both actions become less certain: things that could possibly happen.

- The syntactic structure of the final line remains the same in both versions (the words are in the same order), but the introduction of the question mark changes the clause from a declarative (a statement) to an interrogative (a question). You might note that this seems to cohere with the reduced degree of definiteness in the second version prompted by the changes to the verb phrases.

- There is no right answer as to what the effect of these changes are on the meaning of the poem nor which version is better. However, you might have discussed how these changes to the stylistic features alter your interpretation of the haiku between the two versions.

Chapter 2

Activity 2.3

You can explore the clauses by numbering and describing each sentence in the extract.

1 Multi-clause structure

2 Multi-clause structure

3 Single-clause structure

4 Verbless clause

5 Multi-clause structure

6 Multi-clause structure

7 Verbless clause

8 Multi-clause structure

9 Verbless clause

10 Verbless clause

11 Verbless clause

Across the extract, the multi-clause structures function to build up narrative detail and set the scene for the more emotional response of the narrator when she sees Jack's case. In most instances, the narrator is placed in the subject position of at least one of the clauses so as to give her prominence as a character. Although the entire scene is filtered through her consciousness, the verbless clauses arguably feel more like her thoughts rather than any narrative description. The final three verbless clauses thus reflect her state of mind as she begins to react to her husband's return: their fragmented and direct nature and the final single word 'Disappointment' echo the sudden realisation that she wishes her husband had not yet come back.

Activity 2.4

There are a number of sound patterns that you could comment on here across the two parts (octave and sestet) of this sonnet. For example:

Stanza 1

- The use of alliteration in places to emphasise certain sounds and draw attention to a match between form and meaning, e.g. the repeated /r/ sound in 'rifles' rapid rattle' might evoke and foreground the sound of the guns firing.

- The strategic use of repeated /m/ across the first stanza to foreground particular ideas such as the terrible nature of war and the isolated nature of the soldiers.

- The repetition of fricative /s/, /z/ and /ʃ/ sounds across the stanza to mimic the sounds of the shells.

- The short /æ/ that appears across the first four lines in 'cattle, 'anger', 'rapid', rattle' and 'patter' that provides a sharp punchy rhythm, again mimicking the sounds of the battlefield before the short vowel sounds are replaced by the diphthong /eɪ/in 'hasty', 'save' and 'wail' which have a more drawn out sound.

- The ababcdcd rhyme scheme, which provides a symmetry to the octave.

Stanza 2

- The sestet has a different effegg rhyme scheme, with the final couplet drawing together the emotional 'minds' with the physical 'blinds' to capture the act of those mourning the soldiers away from the battlefield.

- There is more repetition of the fricative set /s/, /z/ and /ʃ/ but also a strong emphasis on plosives to provide a balance between different kinds of sound.

- The movement towards the end of the stanza is from the labial plosive /b/ and the soft palate plosive /g/ to the alveolar plosive /d/ before a final /b/. The final line ends with a plosive + short vowel /d/+/ ʌ/ (dusk) before tailing off with a plosive + diphthong pattern /d/+/ʊə/ (drawing) to /d/+/aʊ/ (down) to /b/ + /aɪ/. The longer vowel sounds encourage a slower, more solemn reading.

Practice question

Here are some of the features of this poem you might have commented on.

- The repetition of 'And', which begins each line and links clauses together (co-ordination).

- The use of the third-person pronoun 'he' rather than a proper noun to both give a sense of familiarity (a pronoun is used when the reader is aware of to whom 'he' refers) and highlight how the character presented might represent us all in terms of having a dual nature.

- The balancing of a verb process denoting a positive action, e.g. 'tucked up' with one that is negative, e.g. 'slippered', to draw attention to the dual nature of the character.

- Informal lexis such as 'quid', again to draw attention to the everyday nature of the character.

- Specific examples, e.g. 'punched', that are foregrounded through internal deviation to highlight the shocking nature of the character's behaviour.

- A simple aaaaccccdddddee rhyme scheme, with the final couplet (the shorter vowel /æ/ in the couplet contrasts with the previous diphthong/long vowel pattern) used to possibly draw attention to the sense of balance in human behaviour that the poem portrays.

- The use of 'they' in subject position of the clause at the end of the poem. Who exactly might 'they' be?

- The parallel structure 'sometimes he did this, sometimes he did that' where the clause pattern reflects the matter-of-fact stance taken towards the character's actions – they are shocking but presented in a way as to suggest they are not entirely surprising or unusual. You could think about what message the poem suggests about human behaviour in light of this.

Chapter 3

Activity 3.1

In this extract, little is presented in direct form. The extract begins with 'He had something to tell her' (NRSA) and 'he announced this the next day', both of which underplay the contents of the speech itself and instead focus on presenting simply that something was said. Two instances of Indirect Speech, 'She asked him if it couldn't wait until after she'd done some work' and 'and he said that there was always something else to do, some other reason to wait and not to talk' are followed by the only example of direct speech in the passage, 'All right, she said […] bring the dogs', although interestingly speech marks are not used, which makes the words feel somehow mediated by the narrator. The final two instances of thought, 'She knew what he wanted to tell her, but she didn't know what he would say', are both indirect, again framed as though under the control of the narrator. Arguably, this pattern of more mediated speech and thought makes the extract feel rather detached, as though we, as readers, are removed from the words and thoughts of the characters themselves.

Activity 3.3

In this extract, you could have highlighted how the old lady is presented through a series of actions (material processes) in which she is the actor as well as through a series of thoughts (mental processes) in which she is the senser. In addition, there are a number of instances where she acts as the sayer in verbal processes. Overall then, she is presented as a well-rounded character afforded a range of verb types to build up a picture for the reader at the beginning of the novel. Interestingly, despite her description as 'the old lady', her agency is emphasised at the end of the extract where she is positioned as the actor in three clauses that have material verb processes: 'There was a slight noise behind her and she turned just in time to seize a small boy by the slack of his roundabout and arrest his flight'.

Activity 3.4

The poem starts with the deictic centre located in the initial speaking voice, the unnamed narrator who encounters the knight-at-arms, describes his physical condition and asks him about his troubles. However, the stanza beginning 'I met a lady in the meads' signals a deictic shift to a new perceptual centre, the knight-at-arms. All subsequent narrative detail in the poem is filtered through this perspective. Indeed this perspective is maintained across the remainder of the poem so that the 'I' never returns to the original narrator. There are shifts in time relaying the knight-at arms' experiences with *la belle dame* but the return to the present tense at the end of the poem is still from the knight-at-arms' perspective. This is unusual since a return to the original framing narrator would be expected. The poem, like the knight-at-arms, seems stranded; interestingly, much literary criticism comments on the puzzling nature of the end of the poem.

Chapter 4

Activity 4.1

A figure-ground analysis can be undertaken at a number of levels of specificity here. At a very superficial level, the main things that form the figure of our attention in this scene are the two characters – 'I', who we discover near the end of the extract is 'Susie', and her father – as well as the snow globe and the penguin. A quick scan over the passage tells us that these objects in the scene are all mentioned more than once – they are repeatedly figured in our attention.

Attention shifts in this passage between the world outside the snow globe, inhabited by Susie and her father, and the world inside the snow globe, inhabited by the penguin. Reflecting on Stockwell's list of attentional attractors, there are multiple attractors within the snow globe which repeatedly encourage the reader to figure the globe's interior: movement, in the form of the snow; brightness in the red and white striped scarf, which also serves to activate a higher degree of 'definiteness' as well as 'brightness'. Far richer detail is given about the inside of the snow globe than the office in which it is situated. The penguin is repeatedly placed in the subject position, giving him a degree of 'activeness' and 'agency': 'Don't worry, Susie, *he* has a nice life. *He's* trapped in a perfect world.' This increases the penguin's 'empathetic recognisability'.

The prepositions also work to direct the reader's attention by offering information about how things are positioned in a scene in relation to each other. This encourages the reader to figure some things and pass quickly over others, leaving them in the ground. This opening to *The Lovely Bones* causes our attention to shift between Susie and her father and the inside of the snow globe. Ultimately the latter forms the main figure of the reader's attention. Consider the first line of the extract: 'Inside the snow globe on my father's desk, there was a penguin [...]'. The prepositions here are 'inside' and 'on' – if unsure, always look for the words that help you work out where things are in relation to each other: 'inside' tells you where the penguin is, 'on' tells you where the snow globe is. Thus, the snow globe does briefly register but the reader is directed to focus not 'on' the snow globe but 'inside' it. Similarly the reader is made aware of Susie's father's desk but their attention is channelled towards the thing 'inside' the thing that's 'on' it. Together these two prepositions push the reader's attention to the penguin. For a while the reader then follows the snow – the world inside the snow globe is fleshed out in richer detail but eventually it falls back 'around' the penguin.

Activity 4.2

There are many potential headers that may activate a schema of 'low intelligence' and thus help the reader to characterise the narrator, Charlie. The spelling is pointedly poor and the use of grammatical conventions within Standard English is erratic. However, closer examination suggests a character who possesses a basic level of literacy and is trying their best to apply their knowledge. For instance, in the phrase 'Miss Kinnians class at the beekmin collidge center for retarted adults' there is inclusion of capitals for Miss Kinnian but absence for the school's name and the possessive apostrophe is missing. Similarly, some spelling is correct but even that which is wrong is approximately phonetically accurate, such as 'collidge' and 'retarted'. This may cause readers to tune their initial schema of 'low intelligence' to one of an eager and effortful protagonist with a learning difficulty. The level of attention to detail in the stylistic rendering of the passage affects the level of tuning likely to take place for individual readers.

The word 'retarted', even with its inaccurate spelling, and in particular its use in the name of the school, may activate a schema for the time period in which the novel is situated: neither contemporary, as the term is no longer considered acceptable in modern usage, nor the very distant past. So too the naming strategies 'Dr', 'perfesser' and 'Miss' may activate medical or education schemas, or perhaps elements of both.

Activity 4.4

In this poem, Hughes draws on the following metaphors:

- LIFE IS A JOURNEY: the speaker talks of life as progression.

- LIFE IS A STAIRCASE: this is a more specific metaphor where the speaker talks of her life as 'Bare' rather than a 'crystal' stair – the staircase metaphor provides a structure for understanding the movement that the addressee needs to make to move from a low point to a high point in terms of social status.

- DIFFICULTIES ARE OBJECTS: difficulties and obstacles in life are portrayed as 'tacks' and 'splinters' to be overcome.

- MOVEMENT IS GOOD AND UP IS GOOD; DOWN IS BAD: these orientational metaphors are used where the speaker talks of 'climbin' and 'reachin' and where the addressee is urged not to 'set down on the steps' and not to 'fall now'.

- LIGHT IS GOOD AND THE KNOWN; DARK IS BAD AND THE UNKNOWN: the speaker presents being in the light as a positive experience and being in the dark as negative and uncertain, 'And sometimes goin' in the dark/Where there ain't been no light'.

Activity 4.6

In the first paragraph, the function-advancing propositions foreground description. The two sentences towards the end of the paragraph, 'The names of the hotels are writ large in neon and weatherproof paint' and 'The word Royal is missing an o', use the verb 'to be' while the verbless clauses that precede them could be understood as elliptical sentences with 'to be' understood. In each case, the scene is simply being described. In the second paragraph, there is a shift to material processes foregrounding action: 'wheel and cry', 'saunter', 'come carrying', 'pausing to put', lean against', 'has blistered and popped', 'picks up' and 'lifts into'. The scene therefore moves from a sense of stillness to rapid movement and urgency. Put simply, it comes to life!

Practice question

In this extract, there is extensive use of negation (which triggers a world-switch). You might have particular ideas about the effect of this pattern, but one possible interpretation is that each negated example represents the gradual movement of the boy towards death. You could develop this pattern into a more fine-tuned analysis of the description of the boy at this stage of the story using the following suggested list of world-switches:

- **Negation:** 'will not come out'

- **Modality:** 'he knows that his sister is in there somewhere'

- **Negation:** 'he cannot find her'

- **Temporal:** 'After thirty minutes'

- **Negation:** 'he doesn't feel cold at all [...] This doesn't seem strange. Nothing seems strange...'

- **Modality:** 'He wants to take his clothes off'

- **Negation:** 'He is not thinking about his sister any more. He cannot remember having a sister'.

References

Bartlett, F.C. (1932) *Remembering: A Study in Experimental and Social Psychology*. Cambridge: Cambridge University Press.

Gavins, J. (2007) *Text World Theory: An Introduction*. Edinburgh: Edinburgh University Press.

Gavins, J. and Steen, G. (2003) *Cognitive Poetics in Practice*. London: Routledge.

Giovanelli, M. (2014) *Teaching Grammar, Structure and Meaning*. London: Routledge.

Gries, S. (2009) 'What is corpus linguistics?', *Language and Linguistics Compass*, 3: 1225–41.

Halliday, M. and Matthiessen, C. (2004) *An Introduction to Functional Grammar* (Third edition). London: Edward Arnold.

Kövecses, Z. (2002) *Metaphor: A Practical Introduction*. New York, NY: Oxford University Press.

Lakoff, G. and Johnson, M. (1980) *Metaphors We Live By*. Chicago, IL: University of Chicago Press.

Lakoff, G. and Turner, M. (1989) *More Than Cool Reason: A Field Guide to Poetic Metaphor*, Chicago, IL: University of Chicago Press.

Leech, G. and Short, M. (2007) *Style in Fiction: A Linguistic Introduction to English Fictional Prose* (Second Edition). London: Longman.

Pope, R. (1995) *Textual Intervention: Critical and Creative Strategies*. London: Taylor and Francis.

Segal, E.M. (1995) 'Narrative comprehension and the role of deictic shift theory'. In J.F. Duchan, G.A. Bruder and L.E. Hewitt (eds) *Deixis in Narrative: A Cognitive Science Perspective*. Hillsdale, NJ: Lawrence Erlbaum, pp. 3–17.

Simpson, P. (1993) *Language, Ideology and Point of View*. London: Routledge.

Simpson, P. (2014) *Stylistics: A Resource Book for Students* (Second Edition). London: Routledge.

Stockwell, P. (2002) *Cognitive Poetics: An Introduction*. London: Routledge.

Stockwell, P. (2009) *Texture: A Cognitive Aesthetics of Reading*, Edinburgh: Edinburgh University Press.

Stockwell, P. (2012) 'The artful science of literary study', *Journal of Foreign Language and Literature (Sichan)*. Original in Chinese (trans. by Juling Ma). Available at: https://goo.gl/FcZ3Ch

Stockwell, P. and Whiteley, S. (eds) (2014) *The Cambridge Handbook of Stylistics*. Cambridge: Cambridge University Press.

Wales, K. (2014) 'The stylistic tool-kit: methods and sub-disciplines'. In P. Stockwell and S. Whiteley (eds) *The Cambridge Handbook of Stylistics*. Cambridge: Cambridge University Press, pp. 32–45.

Werth, P. (1999) *Text Worlds: Representing Conceptual Space in Discourse*. London: Longman.

Glossary

active voice: a clause structure where the agent is placed in subject position for prominence

adjective: a word that modifies a noun

adjective phrase: a group of words that has an adjective as its head word

adverb: a word that modifies a verb, an adjective or another adverb

adverb phrase: a group of words that has an adverb as its head word

affix: the generic term for an addition to a root (a prefix or suffix) which modifies its meaning or creates a new word

agent: the entity responsible for carrying out the verb in an action process

anaphoric referencing: using a word (usually a pronoun) to refer back to a previous, different word so as to create cohesion

antonyms: a word that has an opposite meaning to another word, such as 'happy' and 'sad'

antonymy: a relationship where words have opposite meanings

articulators: parts of the vocal tract that are responsible for producing different types of sound

assonance: a pattern of repeated vowel sounds for effect

attentional attractor: a characteristic of any text element that tends

to encourage a reader to figure something as the focus of their attention

attentional decay: the process by which a figure moves out of the focus of attention and is replaced by a new figure

behavioural process: a process that shows the outward display of some initial internal process

boulomaic modality: expressions that highlight aspects of desire

cataphoric referencing: using a word (usually a pronoun) that refers to another word that follows later

cline: a sliding scale between two extremes where examples can be somewhere in between rather than being one extreme or the other

cognitive poetics: a branch of stylistics concerned with the application of knowledge about how the mind operates to understand the process of literary reading

conceptual metaphor: a structure that presents one concept in terms of another

concordance diagram: a tool offered by corpus programs which allows you to view all the appearances of any word of your choosing in your corpus. In corpus stylistics, your corpus will be a literary text. Concordance diagrams can be organised to display all the words to the left and right of your chosen word either alphabetically or chronologically as they appear in the text

conjunction: a word that connects larger structures such as phrases, clauses and sentences

consent: a person's informed agreement to be researched; in order to give their consent a person needs to know what the research is for and how their responses are going to be used

consent form: a clear and concise document that you will need any readers involved in your project to sign before you begin collecting any of their responses; consent forms should only be signed when a person is in possession of enough information to be accurately informed about what they are giving their consent to

consonance: a pattern of repeated consonant sounds for effect

constituent elements: the particular parts of a phrase or clause

coordinate clause: a clause that is introduced by one of the coordinating conjunctions

corpora: the plural of 'corpus'. A corpus is a collection of words to be examined by the corpus software. It could be a single text or a selection of texts. It will normally contain more text than it is realistically possible for a person to examine and identify patterns without the aid of the software

corpus linguistics: a branch of linguistics that involves the use of computer software to identify patterns across a large amount of text

covert recording: the unethical practice of recording people without their knowledge and consent

defamiliarisation: the process of presenting something in a striking and/or unexpected way

deictic categories: types of deictic expressions (**person, spatial** and **temporal**)

deictic centre: the origin of an expression from which the expression points out and is understood

deictic shift: a movement between particular deictic fields, from one perceptual, temporal and/or spatial centre to another

deixis: words that are context-bound and whose meaning depends on who is using them, and where and when they are being used

deontic modality: expressions that highlight a sense of obligation or necessity

derivational function: the way that an affix helps form a new word by attaching itself to a root

determiner: a word that adds detail or clarity to a noun

deviation: the breaking of textual patterns at any language level

diphthong: a vowel sound that is the combination of two separate sounds, where a speaker moves from one to another

Direct Speech/Thought: speech or thought that is presented word for word but with a speech/thought clause added by the narrator

discourse-world: the context in which communication takes place

distal deixis: deictic expressions that refer to concepts, events or people at a distance from the speaker

epistemic modality: expressions that highlight degrees of belief, certainty or perception

ethical approval: formal permission to carry out a research project, usually granted by a designated person or committee at your school or university

ethical implications: the possible impact a research project could have on any person involved with it, which needs to be carefully considered when designing a study. In particular, any conceivable harm that could be caused to either participants or the researcher themselves must be explored, and addressed, as potential implications of the research

external deviation: deviation that breaks from the normal conventions of language use, for example in the use of nonsense words or ungrammatical constructions

fanfiction: writing inspired by another author's work which borrows elements of the original text

feature spotting: labelling features in a text with metalanguage with no further comment or any reference to the effects that feature creates; a practice to be avoided

figure: whatever forms the current focus of a person's attention

foregrounding: the act of giving some textual features prominence to suggest they have a significant influence on meaning

Free Direct Speech/Thought: speech or thought that is presented word for word with no speech/thought clause added by the narrator

Free Indirect Speech/Thought: speech or thought that is a hybrid of character and narrator representation of what was said

function-advancing propositions: verb processes that drive forward the narrative

Gestalt psychology: an area of research in visual psychology that explores how humans process what they see

ground: elements of any given scene which do not form the current focus of a reader's attention

head word: the main word in the phrase

header: a feature which prompts us to activate certain schemas

hyponomy: a relationship between words where one word is a more specific instance of a more general term

Indirect Speech/Thought: speech or thought that is framed by the narrator but retains an element of what was said by the character

inflectional function: the way that an affix shows a grammatical category such as a verb tense or a plural noun

internal deviation: deviation that breaks from a pattern that has previously been set up in the text for a striking effect

international phonetic alphabet (IPA): a system for showing the different sounds possible

lexical choices: choosing a particular word or phrase

lexis: the term used to refer to the vocabulary system

main clause: a unit in a multi-clause structure that can stand on its own and make complete sense

mapping: the process in which elements of the source domain are structured and understood through corresponding elements in the target domain

meronymy: a relationship between words that have a part-whole structure

metalanguage: terminology used to describe language features

modal auxiliary verb: an auxiliary verb that joins with a main verb to show the degree of commitment towards an event or person that a speaker holds

modal shading: the dominant type of modality in a text

modality: the term used to describe language that presents degrees of attitude or commitment

morphology: the study of word formation

Narrator's Representation of Speech/Thought Act: speech or thought that is presented as a summary by the narrator

Narrator's Representation of Speech/Thought: speech or thought that is presented by the narrator as simply an indication that a character was speaking or thinking

noun: a word that names a thing or concept

noun phrase: a group of words that has a noun as its head word

observer's paradox: a problem whereby a person or group is aware that you are researching what they do or say, and may consciously or unconsciously change their behaviour as a result of being aware that they are being observed

orientational metaphor: a metaphor where a concept is understood through spatial orientation

parallelism: the setting up of textual patterns at any language level

participant information sheet: a clear and concise document that accompanies a consent form giving a person enough information about your project for them to make a decision about whether or not they want to take part; participant information sheets should not exceed two A4 pages

passive voice: a clause structure where the patient is the subject and the agent is omitted or placed later on using a prepositional phrase

patient: the entity directly acted on by the verb in an action process

phoneme: the smallest meaningful distinct unit in the sound system

phonetics: the area of study that is concerned with investigating how sounds are actually produced by language users

phonology: the area of study that refers to the more abstract sound system

prefix: a morpheme that goes before a root word to modify its meaning

pre-modifier: a word that goes before the head noun to add detail or clarify some aspect of it

preposition: a word that shows connections between other words often showing a sense of place or time

prepositional phrase: a group of words that has a preposition as its head word

primary auxiliary verb: an auxiliary verb that joins with a main verb to show tense

principle of text-drivenness: the fact that the text controls the knowledge a reader needs to draw on

pronoun: a word that substitutes for a noun

proximal deixis: deictic expressions that refer to concepts, events or people close to the speaker

reader responses: any record of a reader or readers' thoughts about a text; these could take the form of reviews, comments on an online forum or in a reading group, answers to a questionnaire or even responses in a focus group or interview

real readers: members of the public; this term is usually used to refer to readers outside academia such as researchers, academic experts or literary critics

referent: the concept or thing referred to by a word

research question: a short and clear question which accurately summarises what a study intends to explore: the question to be answered

rewriting exercises: the practice of making deliberate changes to a text, either your own or one by another author, and then reflecting on how those changes have altered the text. Also known as 'textual intervention', a term coined by Rob Pope

rhetoric: the art and study of effective or persuasive speaking or writing

root morpheme: a morpheme that can stand on its own and can usually form a word in its own right

Russian formalism: a movement and literary methodology that aimed to identify the key features of literary texts and account for the unique properties of literary discourse

schema: a bundle of information about something that we hold in our mind

schema accretion: the process by which new facts are added to an existing schema, enlarging its scope and explanatory range

semantic field: a group of words that fulfil the same kind of role and function in speech and writing

semantics: the study of meaning in language

sibilance: a pattern of repeated fricative sounds for effect

sound iconicity: the matching of sound to an aspect of meaning

source domain: a domain of knowledge used as a vehicle for understanding another concept (target domain)

split discourse-world: a discourse-world where participants are separated in time and/or space

stylistics: the study of style; a discipline within the field of linguistics that examines how every linguistic choice can influence the overall effect of a text

subordinate clause: a clause that is introduced by a subordinating conjunction and depends on a main clause to give a complete sense of meaning

suffix: a morpheme that comes after a root word to modify its meaning

synonym: a word that has an equivalent meaning to another word, such as 'happy' and 'joyous'

synonymy: a relationship where words have largely equivalent meanings

syntactic structure: the structure of a sentence

syntax: the study of how words form larger structures such as phrases, clauses and sentences

target domain: the concept that is understood through another domain of knowledge (source domain)

temporal world-switch: a world-switch due to a shift in narrative time

text-world: a rich mental representation that is built up as participants communicate

tuning: the modifications of facts or relations within the schema

verb: a word that shows a state of being, action or event

verb phrase: a group of words that has a verb as its head word

verbal process: a process that presents speech

verbless clause: a clause that does not contain a verb

world-building elements: elements in a text-world that specify time, location, characters and objects

world-switch: a shift that draws attention to a new text-world with different deictic parameters

Index

Acknowledgements

The authors and publishers acknowledge the following sources of copyright material and are grateful for the permissions granted. While every effort has been made, it has not always been possible to identify the sources of all the material used, or to trace all copyright holders. If any omissions are brought to our notice, we will be happy to include the appropriate acknowledgements on reprinting.

Text 2A Extract from the start of poem 'Evening Song' by Kenneth Fearing from *COMPLETE POEMS* by Kenneth Fearing, reprinted by permission of Russell & Volkening as agents for the author. Copyright © 1994 by Jubal Fearing and Phoebe Fearing; Text 2E 'Wind' by Eugen Gomringer (1953); Text 2G from *Funnybones* by Janet Ahlberg and Alan Ahlberg, Puffin Books, Penguin Random House; Text 2H extract from short story 'Dead on the hour' in *A Twist of the Knife*, Pan Macmillan 2014, reproduced with permission of the Licensor (Pan Macmillan) through PLSclear; Text 2L extract from the poem 'The Listeners' Walter de la Mare with permission from The Literary Trustees of Walter de la Mare and The Society of Authors as their representative; Text 2O 'Poem' from *Kid* by Simon Armitage, published by Faber and Faber Ltd, by permission of Faber and Faber Ltd; Figure 4.1 cover of *11.22.63* by Stephen King, Hodder, 2011; Text 4E extract from *Flowers for Algernon* by Daniel Keyes, Gollancz, 2000; Text 4G extract from 'The road not taken' by Robert Frost published by Henry Holt and Penguin Random House Inc.; Text 4H extract from 'I wanna be yours' from *Ten Years in an Open Necked Shirt* by John Cooper Clarke, published by Penguin Random House; Text 4I "Mother to Son" from *THE COLLECTED POEMS OF LANGSTON HUGHES* by Langston Hughes, edited by Arnold Rampersad with David Roessel, Associate Editor, copyright © 1994 by the Estate of Langston Hughes. Used by permission of Alfred A. Knopf, an imprint of the Knopf Doubleday Publishing Group, a division of Penguin Random House LLV. All rights reserved, and with permission from David Higham Associates; Text 5D extract from *Animal Farm* by George Orwell (Copyright © George Orwell, 1945), reprinted by permission of Bill Hamilton as the Literary Executor of the Estate of the Late Sonia Brownell Orwell. Copyright © 1946 by Houghton Mifflin Harcourt Publishing Company and renewed 1974 by Sonia Brownell Orwell. Reprinted by permission of Houghton Mifflin Harcourt Publishing Company. All rights reserved.

Development of this publication has made use of the Cambridge English Corpus (CEC). The CEC is a multi-billion word computer database of contemporary spoken and written English. It includes British English, American English and other varieties of English. It also includes the Cambridge Learner Corpus, developed in collaboration with Cambridge English Language Assessment.

Cambridge University Press has built up the CEC to provide evidence about language use that helps to produce better language teaching materials.

Thanks to the following for permission to reproduce images:

Cover image zdo9/Getty Images, chapter opener images 1-5 Anish Pavitran / EyeEm/Getty Images, Zuzana Janekova / EyeEm/Getty Images, Emmanuel Faure/Getty Images, kelly bowden/Getty Images, webphotographeer/Getty Images

The publisher would like to thank the following members of The Cambridge Panel: English who assisted in reviewing this book: Peter Town, Pramod Kanakath, Obadia Somella, Sagarika Bhatia.